Best New Play in the
for Theatre in Sc

'Harris's electrifying *Oresteia*.' *Guardian* *****

'In Harris's trail-blazing twenty-first-century adaptation there can be no patriarchal ending like the one Aeschylus proposes. Yet Harris's final scene has its own immense civilisational weight.'
Scotsman *****

'A rich, pungent *Oresteia* de nos jours . . . It delivers on its promise in very large measure. Although Harris is largely faithful to Aeschylus' narrative line, she innovates brilliantly . . . Harris writes in a rich, pungent, modern vernacular.'   *Daily Telegraph* ****

'Most fearless of reinventions.'   *Herald* ****

'Zinnie Harris's reworking of Aeschylus' classical trilogy the *Oresteia* imbues that ancient Grecian epic with a merciless modern sensibility . . . Harris's script is a belter: harshly contemporary and eye-wateringly lucid, peeling apart the mechanisations of this ruined family with every word.'   *Exeunt*

'It would be a tragedy to miss it.'
Daily Record ****

'*This Restless House* reimagines the seminal ancient Greek trilogy with invention and dynamism . . . This cocktail of sex and politics is heady and intoxicating.'   *The List*****

A Citizens Theatre production
in association with National Theatre of Scotland

This Restless House

a trilogy of plays by
ZINNIE HARRIS

based on the *Oresteia* by Aeschylus

This Restless House
was first presented in two instalments
at the Citizens Theatre, Glasgow, on 22 and 23 April 2016

This version was first performed at the Citizens Theatre
on 15 August 2017, and co-produced by the Edinburgh
International Festival for the 2017 International Festival

This Restless House

by **Zinnie Harris**

based on the *Oresteia* by Aeschylus

Cast

Agamemnon	**George Anton**
Watchman/Doctor/Jordan	**Peter Collins**
Chorus/Butcher/Michael	**George Costigan**
Chorus/Aegisthus	**Keith Fleming**
Clytemnestra	**Pauline Knowles**
Chorus/Orestes	**Lorn Macdonald**
Cassandra/Celia/Megan	**Itxaso Moreno**
Electra	**Olivia Morgan**
Chorus/Ian	**John O'Mahony**
Ianthe/Audrey	**Kirsty Stuart**
Young Electra	**Chloe Chambers / Orla Hay**
Iphigenia	**Rose Hughes / Freya Kane**
Owen	**Jonas Lennie / Callum McGhie**

Creative Team

Director	**Dominic Hill**
Designer	**Colin Richmond**
Lighting Designer	**Ben Ormerod**
Composer/Sound Designer	**Nikola Kodjabashia**
Movement Director	**EJ Boyle**
Fight Director	**EmmaClaire Brightlyn**
Assistant Director	**Jack Nurse**

All scenery, costumes and props
made in the Citizens Theatre workshop.

Cast

GEORGE ANTON | AGAMEMNON

George trained at the Drama Centre, London.

Theatre credits include: *This Restless House* (Citizens Theatre/National Theatre of Scotland); *Faustus* (Actors Touring Company); *Venice Preserved* (Royal Exchange Theatre); *Don Juan, In the Company of Men* (Royal Shakespeare Company); *The Duchess of Malfi* (Cheek by Jowl); *Life Is A Dream* (Edinburgh International Festival/BAM); *Hamlet* (EIF/Birmingham Rep); *Paul Bright's Confessions of a Justified Sinner* (EIF/Untitled Projects/National Theatre of Scotland); *The Last Witch* (EIF/Traverse Theatre); *Titus Andronicus* (Dundee Rep).

TV credits include: *Marcella, Law and Order: UK* (ITV); *The Loch* (BBC); *The Tudors* (BBC/Showtime); *Robin Hood, Two Thousand Acres of Sky, Seven Industrial Wonders of the World, Hiroshima, Stuart: A Life Backwards* (BBC).

Film credits include: *Calibre* (Wellington Films); *Churchill* (Salon Pictures); *Outlaw* (Pathe); *The Sweeney* (Vertigo); *K-19: The Widowmaker* (First Light Productions); *Field of Vision* (NFTS).

PETER COLLINS | WATCHMAN/DOCTOR/JORDAN

Peter trained at the National Youth Theatre and Royal Central School of Speech and Drama.

Theatre credits include: *Hansel & Gretel, Rapunzel* (Citizens Theatre); *The Story of the Little Gentleman, White, The Ballad of Pondlife McGurk* (Catherine Wheels); *Tin Forest* (National Theatre of Scotland); *Horizontal Collaboration* (David Leddy/Fire Exit); *Caucasian Chalk Circle* (Complicite/National Theatre); *Much Ado About Nothing, The Taming of the Shrew* (Royal Exchange Theatre); *How the Other Half Loves* (Octagon Theatre Bolton); *Northern Exposure* (Paines Plough); *Macbeth, Thebans, Medea, King Lear, Julius Caesar, Romeo and Juliet, Hamlet* (Babel Theatre); *The Tempest* (Compass Theatre); *Beauty and the Beast* (Tron Theatre); *Hamlet: First Cut* (Red Shift); *Temptations and Betrayals* (Bristol Old Vic); *Grimm Tales* (Haymarket Theatre, Leicester).

Television and radio credits include: *Scot Squad* (Comedy Unit/BBC Scotland); *The Secret Agent* (World Productions/BBC); *Eve* (Leopard Productions/CBBC); *The Hunt* (Carlton); *Always and Everyone* (Granada); *Peak Practice* (ITV); *Casualty* (BBC) and *Lulu's Back in Town* (BBC Scotland).

GEORGE COSTIGAN | CHORUS/BUTCHER/MICHAEL

For the Citizens Theatre: *This Restless House* (2016); *Crime and Punishment* (2013).

Other theatre in Scotland includes: George in John Steinbeck's *Of Mice and Men* (King's Theatre, Edinburgh); *Trust Byron* (Edinburgh Festival Fringe, 1998, nominated for Best Actor); Claudius in Calixto Bietio's production of *Hamlet* (Edinburgh International Festival, 2003); David Harrower's *Blackbird* (Tron Theatre, 2011).

Film credits include: *The Hawk* directed by David Hayman, and *Summer* directed by Kenny Glenaan. George also once compered three nights of freestyle wrestling in Aberdeen. Never again.

KEITH FLEMING | AEGISTHUS/CHORUS

Theatre credits include: *Para Handy* (Pitlochry Festival Theatre); *The Breakfast Plays, The Dark Things, Pandas* (Traverse); *The Lonesome West* (Tron Theatre); *Dunsinane* (National Theatre of Scotland USA tour, UK tour with the RSC); *The Venetian Twins, Union* (Royal Lyceum Theatre Edinburgh); *This Restless House* (Citizens Theatre/National Theatre of Scotland); *Vanya, Miss Julie* (Citizens Theatre); *What Goes Around* (Cumbernauld Theatre); *City of the Blind* (Fire Exit); *Macbeth* (Perth Theatre); *Beautiful Burnout* (Frantic Assembly); *Squash, Call of the Wild, An Incident at the Border* (Òran Mór); *Barflies* (Grid Iron); David Leddy's *Untitled Love Story* and *Doubt*; *Days Of Wine and Roses* (Theatre Jezebel); *Black Watch, The Miracle Man, The Making of Us* (National Theatre of Scotland); *Peer Gynt* (National Theatre of Scotland/Dundee Rep).

Television credits include: *Outlander* (Starz/Tall Ship Productions); *West Skerra Light* (BBC/Hopscotch Films).

PAULINE KNOWLES | CLYTEMNESTRA

Pauline recently appeared in *Wee Free! The Musical* (Òran Mór); *Hay Fever* (Citizens Theatre); *Jumpy* (Royal Lyceum Theatre Edinburgh), directed by Cora Bissett, and *This Restless House* (Citizens Theatre/National Theatre of Scotland), directed by Dominic Hill, for which she won the CATS award for Best Female Performance.

Theatre credits include: *Threads* (Stellar Quines); *Lot and His God, Othello, Cinderella, Wizard of Oz, Liar* (Citizens Theatre); *Marilyn* (Citizens Theatre/Royal Lyceum Theatre Edinburgh); *The Lion, the Witch and the Wardrobe, A Christmas Carol* (Royal Lyceum Theatre Edinburgh); *The Garden* (Sound Festival); *While You Lie* (Traverse); *Crazy Jane* (Birds of Paradise); *The Effect* (Firebrand Theatre); *A Slow Air* (Borderline Theatre); *Some Other Mother* (AJ Taudevin); *The Government Inspector* (Communicado Theatre); *Fleeto, Wee Andy* (Tumult in the Clouds); *Pass the Spoon* (Magnetic North).

TV and radio credits include: *Case Histories* (Ruby Films/BBC); *Personal Affairs* (2AMTV/BBC); *Garrow's Law* (Shed/BBC); *Manhunters* (BBC); *Taggart* (STV); *Autumn Princess* (BBC).

LORN MACDONALD | CHORUS/ORESTES

Lorn graduated in 2015 from the Royal Conservatoire of Scotland.

Theatre credits include: *Trainspotting* (Citizens Theatre); *This Restless House* (Citizens Theatre/National Theatre of Scotland); *Boys* (Soho Theatre/Nuffield Theatre/Headlong/Hightide Festival Theatre); *What We Know* (Traverse Theatre).

TV credits include: *World's End* (BBC); *Neverland* (Sky Movies/Syfy); *Outlander* (Starz/Tall Ship Productions).

Radio credits include: *Boswell at Large: A Corsican Adventure* (BBC)

Film credits include: *Beats* (Sixteen Films).

ITXASO MORENO | CASSANDRA/CELIA/MEGAN

Itxaso trained at BAI (Bizkaia Drama School) in Bilbao, Basque Country.

Theatre credits include: *Everyman, Nation* (National Theatre); *Crude* (Grid Iron); *Out of This World* (V-TOL); *Three's A Crowd* (All Or Nothing); *Horizontal Collaboration* (Fire Exit); *The Tale o' Fanny Cha Cha* (Òran Mór/Lemon Tree); *Perch: Carnival of Flying and Falling* (Conflux); *The Arabian Nights* (Tricycle Theatre, London); *The Tempest* (Theatre Royal Haymarket); *The Legend of Captain Crow's Teeth* (Unicorn Theatre, London); *Peter Pan* (ThreeSixty Entertainment); *Amada, Horses Horses Running in All Directions* (The Arches); *Yarn* (Grid Iron/Dundee Rep); *Fermentation, Once upon a Dragon* (Grid Iron); *Roam* (Grid Iron/National Theatre of Scotland); *Home* (National Theatre of Scotland); *Green Whale* (Licketyspit Theatre); *Trojan Women* (Theatre Cryptic); *Lost Ones, Invisible Man, Stars Beneath the Sea* (Vanishing Point); *Red* (Boilerhouse).

TV credits include: *Rebus: The Naming of the Dead* (STV).

Film credits include: *Two Donuts* (FIN Productions).

OLIVIA MORGAN | ELECTRA

Olivia trained at the Royal Academy of Dramatic Art.

Theatre credits include: *This Restless House* (Citizens Theatre/National Theatre of Scotland); *Brave New World* (Royal & Derngate Northampton/Touring Consortium); *Offside* (Futures Theatre); *The Taming of the Shrew* (Shakespeare's Globe); *Macbeth* (Ambassador Theatre Group); *The Serpent's Tooth* (Almeida Theatre/Talawa Theatre Company); *The Charity That Began at Home* (Orange Tree Theatre); *King Lear* (West Yorkshire Playhouse).

TV credits include: *Outlander* (Starz/Tall Ship Productions); *Hereafter* (Kudos); *Holby City, Doctors* (BBC); *Tracey Ullman's Show* (BBC); *Tracey Breaks The News* (BBC); *The Loch* (ITV).

Radio credits include: *Suddenly, a Stranger* (BBC Scotland); Walter Scott trilogy (Pacificus Productions).

Film credits include: *Calibre* (Wellington Films); *Dartmoor Killing* (Hummingbird Films); *Murmur* (Little Northern Light/Lunar Lander Films).

JOHN O'MAHONY | CHORUS/IAN

Theatre credits include: *Hansel & Gretel, A Christmas Carol* (Citizens Theatre); *Puckoon* (Big Telly, Leicester Square Theatre); *Dracula, Copenhagen, Alphabetical Order* (New Vic Theatre); *As You Like It* (Shakespeare's Globe); *The Pillowman*

(Norwich Theatre Royal); *Treasure Island* (Rose Theatre, Kingston); *The Tempest* (Regent's Park Open Air Theatre); *Fly in the Ointment, Cover Her Feet* (Stephen Joseph Theatre); *Twelfth Night, Macbeth* (Exeter Northcott Theatre); *Death of a Salesman* (European tour); *Belonging* (Birmingham Rep); *Moby Dick* (European tour); *Buddy* (National tour); *A Midsummer Night's Dream, Cider With Rosie, Corpse for Sale, Moll Flanders* (Derby Theatre); *Boots for the Footless* (Tricycle Theatre); *Great Expectations* (The Old Vic); *Up in the Gallery* (national tour).

Television and film credits include: *Good Karma Hospital* (Tiger Aspect); *Miracle Landing on the Hudson* (National Geographic); *Doctors, Mrs Brown's Boys, Judge John Deed, Murphy's Law* (BBC); *Law and Order* (Kudos); *Dirty Filthy Love* (Granada); *Babel* (Paramount); *Bad Girls* (Shed Productions); *A Short Film about John Bolton* (SKA Films); *TLC* (Positive TV); *Father Ted* (Hat Trick); *The Chief* (Anglia Television).

Radio credits include: *Cabin Pressure, Scummow, After the Break, Anzacs Over England, The Absentee, The Babel Philosopher* (BBC).

KIRSTY STUART | IANTHE/AUDREY

Kirsty trained at Drama Centre London.

Theatre credits include: *Crude* (Grid Iron); *The Girl in the Machine* (Traverse); *Flo, Thoughts Spoken Aloud From Above, Tristan Nightaway* (Òran Mór); *Uncanny Valley* (Ayr Gaiety/Edinburgh International Science Festival); *Fever Dream: Southside* (Citizens Theatre); *Molly Whuppie, Licketyleap* (Licketyspit); *Silence of the Bees* (The Arches); *The Infamous Brothers Davenport* (Vox Motus/ Royal Lyceum Theatre Edinburgh); *The Hunted* (Visible Fictions); *Romeo and Juliet* (Open Book); *Spring Awakening* (Grid Iron/Traverse Theatre); *I Was a Beautiful Day* (Tron Theatre/Finborough Theatre); *Fast Labour* (West Yorkshire Playhouse/Hampstead Theatre).

Screen credits include: *River City* (BBC Scotland); *Lip Service* (Kudos); *Closing the Ring* (CTR/Premiere Picture); *Doctors, Sea of Souls* (BBC).

Creative Team

ZINNIE HARRIS | AUTHOR

Zinnie Harris is a playwright, screenwriter and theatre director. Her plays include the multi-award-winning *Further than the Furthest Thing* (National Theatre/Tron Theatre – winner of the 1999 Peggy Ramsay Award, 2001 John Whiting Award, Fringe First Award), *How to Hold Your Breath* (Royal Court Theatre – joint winner of the Berwin Lee Award), *The Wheel* (National Theatre of Scotland – joint winner of the 2011 Amnesty International Freedom of Expression Award, Fringe First Award), *Nightingale and Chase* (Royal Court Theatre), *Midwinter, Solstice* (both RSC), *Fall* (Traverse Theatre/RSC) and *By Many Wounds* (Hampstead Theatre). Her stage adaptations include Ibsen's *A Doll's House* for the Donmar Warehouse and Strindberg's *Miss Julie* for the National Theatre of Scotland.

Zinnie received an Arts Foundation Fellowship for Playwriting, and was Writer in Residence at the RSC, 2000 –2001. She has directed for the RSC, Traverse Theatre, Tron Theatre and Royal Lyceum Theatre, winning Best Director in the 2017 Critics' Awards for Theatre in Scotland for her production of Caryl Churchill's *A Number*. She has written for television including episodes for the BBC1 Drama series *Spooks*, and two standalone television films for Channel 4. She is Professor of Playwriting and Screenwriting at the University of St Andrews, and an Associate Director at the Traverse Theatre.

DOMINIC HILL | DIRECTOR

Dominic Hill is Artistic Director of the Citizens Theatre. Since joining the Citizens in 2011, he has directed *Hay Fever, Hansel & Gretel, The Rivals, This Restless House* (winner of Best Director, 2016 CATS Awards), *Endgame, The Choir, Fever Dream: Southside, A Christmas Carol, Hamlet, The Libertine, Miss Julie, Crime and Punishment* (winner of Best Director and Best Production, 2014 CATS Awards), *Far Away, Seagulls, Doctor Faustus, Sleeping Beauty, Krapp's Last Tape, Footfalls, King Lear* and *Betrayal* (winner of Best Director, 2012 CATS Awards).

Before joining the Citizens he was Artistic Director of the Traverse Theatre in Edinburgh and Joint Artistic Director of Dundee Rep. Other credits include *Falstaff* and *Macbeth* (Scottish Opera) and *The City Madam* (Royal Shakespeare Company). He has directed in theatres in London and throughout the UK.

COLIN RICHMOND | DESIGNER

Colin trained at the Royal Welsh College of Music and Drama, Cardiff graduating with First Class BA Hons. He won the Lord Williams Design Award 2002 and 2003, and in 2003 was a Linbury Prize Finalist. Colin has been nominated twice for the Critics' Awards for Theatre in Scotland (CATS) for best design for *Betrayal* at Citizens Theatre and for *Sweeney Todd* at Dundee Rep Theatre. Colin was made a Companion of Liverpool Institute of Performing Arts in 2014.

Productions include: *This Restless House, Doctor Faustus, Crime and Punishment* (Citizens Theatre); *This Annie* (West End and UK tour); *Jimmy's Hall* (Abbey Theatre, Dublin); *Into the Woods* (Opera North/West Yorkshire Playhouse); *After Miss Julie* (Bath Theatre Royal); *Pinocchio* (National Ballet of Canada); *Antony and Cleopatra* (Shakespeare's Globe); *Titus Andronicus, Wendy and Peter Pan, Breakfast with Mugabe* (Royal Shakespeare Company); *Pressure* (Chichester Festival Theatre/Royal Lyceum Theatre Edinburgh); *Kiss Me Kate* (Opera North/ Welsh National Opera); *Beautiful Thing, Breakfast with Mugabe, Bad Girls: The Musical, Entertaining Mr Sloane, Ring Round the Moon* (West End); *Europe* (Barbican); *Men Should Weep, Yer Granny* (National Theatre of Scotland); *Animal Farm, Christmas Carol, Billy Liar* (West Yorkshire Playhouse); *La bohème, Don Pasquale* (Opera Holland Park); *Twelfth Night, Betrayal* (Crucible Sheffield); *Spring Awakening, Restoration* (Headlong); *My Fair Lady* (Denmark); *The Three Musketeers and the Princess of Spain* (English Touring Theatre/Traverse Theatre); *Grease* (Curve/World Trade Centre, Dubai).

BEN ORMEROD | LIGHTING DESIGNER

Previous productions at the Citizens Theatre include *King Lear* and *Hamlet*.

Theatre credits include: *Woyzeck in Winter* (Landmark Productions/Galway International Arts Festival/Barbican); *The Happiness Project* (Umanoove); *A Number* (Royal Lyceum Theatre Edinburgh); *Mrs Henderson Presents* (Theatre Royal Bath/Michael Harrison Entertainment, West End/ Toronto); *The Tempest* (Print Room); *Trouble in Mind, The One That Got Away, Things We Do for Love, Intimate Apparel, Spanish Golden Age season* (Theatre Royal Bath, Ustinov Studio); *Donegal* (Abbey Theatre, Dublin); *The Libertine* (Theatre Royal Bath and West End); *Fings Ain't Wot They Used t'Be* (Theatre Royal Stratford East); *Onassis, Macbeth* (West End); *Zorro* (West End, US, Japan, Netherlands); *The Beauty Queen of Leenane* (Druid/Royal Court, Broadway, Toronto, Sydney); the Spanish Golden Age season (Royal Shakespeare Company); *In Remembrance of Things Past, The Colleen Bawn* (National Theatre).

Opera and dance credits include: *Tristan und Isolde, Tannhäuser, Der Ring des Nibelungen* (Longborough Festival Opera); *Three Dancers* (Rambert); *See Blue Through* (Phoenix Dance Theatre); *A Mighty Wind* (National Dance Company Wales); *Casse-Noisette, Les Noces* (Grand Théâtre de Genève); *La traviata* (Danish National Opera); *Carmen* (Lithuania National Ballet) and productions for Scottish Opera, English National Opera, Ballet Gulbenkian, Accademia Nazionale di Santa Cecilia in Rome, Candoco and Walker Dance Park Music. Ben is lighting consultant for the Calico Museum of Textiles, Ahmedabad; directed Athol Fugard's *Dimetos* (Gate Theatre) and adapted four films from Kieślowski's *Dekalog* for E15.

NIKOLA KODJABASHIA | COMPOSER/SOUND DESIGNER

Nikola Kodjabashia is considered to be one of the most eminent representatives of the Balkan and Eastern European musical avant-garde today.

Theatre credits include: *Hansel & Gretel, This Restless House, A Christmas Carol, Hamlet, Crime and Punishment* (Citizens Theatre); *La Suite* (Fabien Prioville Dance Company with support from Pina Bausch Foundation); Musical Director for Sir Peter Hall's production of Sir Harrison Birtwistle's *Bacchai* (National Theatre); *Kafka's Monkey* (Young Vic); *The Three Musketeers and the Princess of Spain* (English Touring Theatre/Traverse Theatre); *Inkheart, Romeo and Juliet* (HOME, Manchester); *Out of Blixen, Scherzo for Piano and Stick, Insomnia* (Riotous Theatre Company); *Siege* (Freedom Theatre); Wajdi Mouawad's *Scorched* (Old Vic); *Hecuba* (Donmar Warehouse).

Commissions include: scores for La Biennale di Venezia 2004, BBC Singers 2010, National Theatre 2002/3, Macedonian National Opera and Ballet 2013, Macedonian Philharmonic Orchestra 2009, Moscow Contemporary Music Ensemble 1999.

TV and film credits include: music for the award-winning film *Defining Fay* (Orev); *Dear Anna* (November Films); *Racism: a History, Gothica* (BBC); *Saints,*

Dance with Me and *Green Pages* (BBC/Arena); *Grandmothers of the Revolution* (Petra Pan Productions Slovenia).

Radio credits include: *Massistonia* (BBC Radio).

Recordings include: *Reveries of the Solitary Walker, The Most of Now, Explosion of a Memory* (Live with Macedonian Philharmonic Orchestra) *Penelope X*. His music is released by ReR, described by the *Guardian* as 'one of the most adventurous and coherent of avant-rock labels'.

EJ BOYLE | MOVEMENT DIRECTOR

Theatre credits include: *Cuttin' a Rug, This Restless House, Trainspotting, Sports Day* (Citizens Theatre); *Lanark: A Life in Three Acts* (Edinburgh International Festival/Citizens Theatre); *Richard III* (West Yorkshire Playhouse); *Hedda Gabler, Jumpy, The Lion, the Witch and the Wardrobe* (Royal Lyceum Theatre Edinburgh); *The Cheviot, the Stag and the Black Black Oil, Great Expectations, James and the Giant Peach, The BFG, Victoria* (Dundee Rep); *Not About Heroes* (Eden Court); *Still Game: Live* (Glasgow Hydro); *Forest Boy* (Arcola/Royal Conservatoire of Scotland/Noisemaker); *Cabaret, West Side Story, Carousel, Tommy* (Royal Conservatoire of Scotland).

TV and film credits include: *The Crown* (Netflix Original Series); *God Help the Girl* (Sundance Film Festival 2014 Special Jury Prize); *Two Doors Down* (STV); *In Plain Sight* (ITV).

Other work includes: Creative Associate and Choreographer, Glasgow 2014 Commonwealth Games Ceremonies; Mass Movement Director, The Queen's 90th Birthday Patron's Parade; Assistant Artistic Director, Baku 2015 European Games; Director, *Under the Ground* (Edinburgh Festival Fringe); Associate Director, *Out of This World* (Sadler's Wells/tour).

EMMACLAIRE BRIGHTLYN | FIGHT DIRECTOR

Originally from Canada, EmmaClaire Brightlyn is a freelance actress, fight director and teacher based in Glasgow. As well as regularly teaching for the Royal Conservatoire of Scotland, EmmaClaire was part of the first ever International Stage Combat Workshop in Toronto, Canada, in 2016, and was a guest panelist at the 25th Anniversary International Paddy Crean Workshop in Banff, Canada, in January 2017.

Fight directing credits include: *Dragon* (Vox Motus/National Theatre of Scotland/Tianjin Children's Art Theatre); *West Side Story, Festen, Brigadoon* (Royal Conservatoire of Scotland); *The Maids, Miss Julie, The Libertine, Rapunzel, This Restless House* (Citizens Theatre); *The Lonesome West* (Tron Theatre); *The Seafarer, Macbeth* (Perth Theatre); *Hamlet* (Wilderness of Tigers); *Slope* (Untitled Projects); *Titus Andronicus* (Dundee Rep). EmmaClaire also appeared as a featured Gladiator and co-fight captain in *Ben Hur Live!* (New Arts Concerts, Germany) in 2011. Most recently EmmaClaire has been Fight Arranger on Scottish feature films *Anna and the Apocalypse* (Blazing Griffin) and *Beats* (Sixteen Films).

She has taught physical theatre and stage combat for the Royal Conservatoire of Scotland, Edinburgh College, various Stagecoach groups and at the University of Lethbridge in Canada.

JACK NURSE | ASSISTANT DIRECTOR

Jack is a director and theatre-maker and trained at the Royal Conservatoire of Scotland. In 2014 he co-founded Wonder Fools, a Glasgow-based theatre company.

For Wonder Fools, directing credits include: *549: Scots of the Spanish Civil War*, *McNeill of Tranent: Fastest Man in the World* and *The Coolidge Effect*.

Other directing credits include: *O* (Royal Conservatoire of Scotland); *Too Fast* (Fullarton Theatre) and *Sparkleshark* (Fullarton Theatre and Ryan Centre).

As an assistant director, credits include: *Blackbird* (Citizens Theatre); *The Winter's Tale* (Royal Lyceum Theatre Edinburgh); *Hay Fever* (Citizens Theatre/ Royal Lyceum Theatre Edinburgh), *The Broons* (Selladoor Worldwide), for which he was also Staff Director on its Scottish tour. Wonder Fools are one of six Graduate Emerging Companies at the New Diorama Theatre. Jack is one of ten emerging directors in the Almeida Theatre's Directors' Pool.

The Citizens Company

Thomas Abela — Front of House
Neil Anderson — Technician
Amy Angus — Drama Class Tutor
Fin Bain — Front of House
Paul C Bassett — Front of House Duty Manager
Catherine Bird — Payroll Officer
Ashleigh Blair — Assistant Scenic Artist
Marissa Bonnar — Front of House
Alex Brady — Box Office Supervisor/IT
Suzanne Brady — Box Office/Drama Class Tutor
Laura Briggs — Front of House
Louise Brown — Creative Learning Officer
Andrew Bunton — Front of House
Theo Cherry — Front of House
Jen Clokey — Drama Class Tutor
Steph Connell — Stage One Producer
Lisa Corr — Drama Class Tutor
Natalia Cortes — Company Stage Manager
Peter Cowan — Box Office
Elaine G. Coyle — Head of Wardrobe
Carol Cull — Housekeeper
Caroline Darke — Trusts and Foundations Manager
Lesley Davidson — General Manager
Saul Davidson — Front of House
Denise Differ — Box Office Manager
Louise Dingwall — Press and Marketing Officer
Michael Dorrance — Deputy Head of Workshop
Ann Dundas — Housekeeper
Lisa Dundas — Finance Assistant
Paul Dundas — Front of House Manager
Sophie Fernie — Front of House
Robyn Ferguson — Box Office
Joanne Ferrie — Tree Fabrication
Clara Fink — Tree Fabrication
Archie Fisher — Front of House
Barry Forde — Assistant Stage Manager
Neil Francis — Drama Class Tutor
Ben Frost — Wardrobe Assistant
Jacky Gardiner — Front of House
Harvey Gardner — Front of House
Anne Gillan — Finance Officer

Elly Goodman — Community Drama Artist
Maddy Grant — Deputy Stage Manager
Jessica Griffiths — Wardrobe Assistant Dresser
Davy Harrop — Front of House/ Stage Door Administrator
Stephen Harrop — Front of House Duty Manager
Jamie Hayes — Head of Stage
Neil Haynes — Head Scenic Artist
Dominic Hill — Artistic Director
Neil Hobbs — Deputy Head of Lighting and Sound
Guy Hollands — Associate Director (Citizens Learning)
Olivia Hughes — Front of House
Caroline James — Drama Class Tutor
Miles Jarvis — Front of House
Euan Jenkins — Front of House
Stuart Jenkins — Head of Lighting and Sound
Arthur Johnston — Front of House/ Stage Door Administrator
Simon Jones — Stage Door Administrator
Niamh Kane — Front of House
Judith Kilvington — Executive Director
Sarah Kinsey — Wardrobe Assistant
Jenny Knotts — Box Office
Campbell Lawrie — Paul Hamlyn Club Co-ordinator/Drama Class Supervisor
Jamie Leary — Front of House/Box Office
Karen Lee-Barron — Wardrobe Assistant/ Dresser
Stuart Leech — Technician
Gary Loughran — Tree Fabrication
Alison MacKinnon — Head of Marketing and Communications
Rose Manson — Front of House
Collette Marshall — Front of House
Carly McCaig — Community Drama Worker
Erin McCardie — Front of House
Sarah McGavin — Drama Class Tutor
Morna McGeogh — Drama Class Tutor
Michael McGurk — Front of House

The Citizens Theatre is Glasgow's major producing theatre and one of the leading theatre companies in the UK. Based in a beautiful Victorian theatre dating from 1878 in the Gorbals area of Glasgow, it is led by Artistic Director, Dominic Hill and Executive Director, Judith Kilvington.

The Citizens has a distinguished history spanning over 70 years and has built an international reputation for producing dynamic and innovative work, centered on bold new interpretations of classic texts. Productions on stage are presented alongside a highly regarded programme of participatory and education work, with a special emphasis on work with children, young people and socially excluded adults. As its name suggests, the Citizens Theatre believes that theatre can enhance and transform the lives of people of all ages, cultures and social backgrounds.

The theatre is currently planning and fundraising for a transformative multimillion pound capital project which will be the first comprehensive, integrated redevelopment of the building in its 139-year history.

For the latest information on all Citizens Theatre shows, learning and participation activity and the forthcoming theatre redevelopment project visit:

citz.co.uk

Citizens Theatre, 119 Gorbals Street, Glasgow, G5 9DS
Box Office: 0141 429 0022 | Admin: 0141 429 5561

Citizens Theatre Ltd. Registered No. SC022513
and is a Scottish Charity No.SC001337

This Restless House

Zinnie Harris's plays include the multi-award-winning *Further than the Furthest Thing* (National Theatre/Tron Theatre; winner of the 1999 Peggy Ramsay Award, 2001 John Whiting Award, Edinburgh Fringe First Award), *How to Hold Your Breath* (Royal Court Theatre; joint winner of the Berwin Lee Award), *The Wheel* (National Theatre of Scotland; joint winner of the 2011 Amnesty International Freedom of Expression Award; Fringe First Award), *Nightingale and Chase* (Royal Court Theatre), *Midwinter*, *Solstice* (both RSC), *Fall* (Traverse Theatre/RSC), *By Many Wounds* (Hampstead Theatre) and *Meet Me at Dawn* (Traverse Theatre). Her adaptations include Ibsen's *A Doll's House* for the Donmar Warehouse and Strindberg's *Miss Julie* for the National Theatre of Scotland. Zinnie received an Arts Foundation Fellowship for playwriting, and was Writer in Residence at the RSC, 2000–2001. She is Professor of Playwriting and Screenwriting at St Andrews University, and an Associate Director at the Traverse Theatre.

also by Zinnie Harris from Faber

ZINNIE HARRIS

This Restless House

a trilogy of plays based around
the *Oresteia* by Aeschylus

with an introduction by
Charlotte Higgins

FABER & FABER

First published in 2016
by Faber and Faber Ltd
74–77 Great Russell Street
London WC1B 3DA

This revised edtion 2017

Typeset by Country Setting, Kingsdown, Kent CT14 8ES
Printed in England by CPI Group (UK) Ltd, Croydon CR0 4YY

A CIP record for this book
is available from the British Library

978-0-571-33262-5

FSC
www.fsc.org
MIX
Paper from
responsible sources
FSC® C013604

4 6 8 10 9 7 5

Contents

Acknowledgements

My thanks go to Frances Poet, George Aza-Selinger, Jasper Harris, George Costigan, Kathryn Howden, Finlay Welsh, Lucianne McEvoy, Ron Donachie, Ian Dunn and Jessica Hardwick for their insightful support developing the scripts though various drafts and workshops.

Thanks also to Professor Stephen Halliwell for his reading list on ancient Greek tragedy and his encouragement.

Brice Avery, I am indebted to you for the hours spent in your study talking about attachment, trauma and what goes wrong in families from a psychoanalytic point of view. (I have possibly misrepresented your wisdom but I hope you will accept a theatrical spin!)

Steve King, I am grateful for all your hard work at Faber making this publication happen.

Thanks also to Laurie Sansom for the support and faith in the project from the early days and for commissioning the scripts, to the NTS for their enthusiasm and energies as a co-producer, and all at the Citizens Theatre for the commitment and hard work to make this happen.

Above all a huge thanks to Dominic Hill for all his precision, belief and brilliance.

This Restless House was first presented at the Citizens Theatre, Glasgow, on 22 April 2016.

Agamemnon George Anton
Watchman / Doctor / Jordan Adam Best
Chorus / Ian Cliff Burnett
Chorus/Butcher / Michael George Costigan
Chorus / Aegisthus Keith Fleming
Clytemnestra Pauline Knowles
Chorus / Orestes Lorn MacDonald
Cassandra / Celia / Megan Itxaso Moreno
Electra Olivia Morgan
Ianthe / Audrey Anita Vettesse
Young Electra Chloe Chambers / Orla Hay
Iphigenia Rose Hughes / Freya Kane
Owen Jonas Lennie / Callum McGhie

Director Dominic Hill
Designer Colin Richmond
Lighting Designer Ben Ormerod
Composer / Sound Designer Nikola Kodjabashia
Movement Director E.J. Boyle
Fight Director EmmaClaire Brightlyn
Assistant Director Jack Nurse

In the present revised version it was first performed at the Citizens Theatre on 15 August 2017, and was also presented at the Edinburgh International Festival 2017.

Introduction

by Charlotte Higgins

What would it take for you to stab to death someone
you desperately loved? This is the question that lies at
the heart of Zinnie Harris's adaptation of Aeschylus'
Oresteia, the trilogy of dramas first produced in Athens
in 458 BC. In its first part, the King of Argos comes
home; he has, after a decade-long siege, finally defeated
and destroyed the city of Troy. But on the threshold of his
restoration to family life the victorious general is defeated
and downed by his wife, slashed to death in the bath. For
Aeschylus, Clytemnestra is an impressively powerful, but
inescapably terrifying, even barbaric figure: rhetorically
able, persuasive and murderous. Harris, on the other
hand, while reducing none of Clytemnestra's power, has
dug into her interior; in so doing she takes us step by step
through the mind of a wife who becomes a husband-
killer – a mind that has become clotted with grief and
rage towards a man who first sacrificed their own child to
secure from the gods a fair wind to Troy, and then brought
back a war-looted concubine to share the marital home.

This particular strategy of Harris's – to edge us towards
the interior lives of Aeschylus' characters, of her characters,
while losing none of the shock of their external actions –
leads her into intriguing territory. Aeschylus' plays – the
only complete trilogy to have survived from antiquity –
begin with a horrific, seemingly uncontrollable cycle of
killing and revenge. The second play, *The Libation
Bearers*, has Clytemnestra killed by her son, Orestes, in
revenge for Agamemnon's death. Orestes is at once beset
by the Furies, the mad-making, terror-spreading creatures
who pursue murderers.

In Aeschylus' third, *The Kindly Ones*, Orestes, still pursued by the Furies, is brought to Athens and tried for his crime. The goddess Athena appears to preside over the court; the god Apollo becomes Orestes' counsel. The jury of citizens is equally split; Athena exercises the casting vote to acquit the defendant on the supremely sexist grounds that the murder of a mother is a lesser crime than the murder of a husband. (The somewhat casuistical reasoning is that the mother in carrying the foetus acts only as its 'container', so is not really a family member. The play, wrote Simone de Beauvoir in *The Second Sex*, 'represents the triumph of the patriarchate over the matriarchate'.) The trial having been concluded, the Furies must be somehow dealt with: and so they are transformed by Athena into 'kindly ones', their violence tamed and neutered.

This third play had a very particular resonance when it was premiered. The court at which Orestes is tried is called the Areopagus. The body existed in Aeschylus' day; traditionally, it had had important legislative powers and was strongly aristocratic in its make-up. But the politician Ephialtes, who had been assassinated three years before the play's premiere, deprived it of all its functions save that of a homicide court – an important step in creating Athenian radical democracy. *The Kindly Ones* imagines Orestes' trial as the first and founding event to be conducted by the body, and, therefore gives the Areopagus' reduced powers an important mythological aetiology, while hinting that its other functions had been inauthentic accretions. *The Kindly Ones*, then – the only Greek tragedy to unfold in a kingless city – is a play about democracy, and what must become of a democracy's most violent, troubling elements. It is important that the Furies are subsumed into the city – to live, literally, beneath it, as if they were become the community's suppressed unconscious. Their role of terrorising murderers is removed from them, and given to the state judiciary.

Harris's encounter with Aeschylus' text, however, has taken her down a slightly different path. For her, Clytemnestra's daughters become pivotal – both Iphigenia, the child who was killed by Agamemnon before the Trojan war, and the one at home, Electra. In her second play, *The Bough Breaks*, we are plunged into the second daughter's mind, as she grows up in the tainted, claustro-phobic household of Clytemnestra and her lover, Aegisthus. (In this way, Harris's play has a family relationship with Strauss's expressionist opera *Elektra*.) She loves, almost worships her mother; but the return of Orestes after a long absence breaks this deep attachment, or rather illusion. In Harris's play, it is Electra, not Orestes, who wields the knife. Guilt and discomfort, pain and confusion, pervade the play. Harris, playing with the internal–external manifestations of this chain of horror, has her characters plagued by odd itches, mysterious ailments, strange hallucinations. Perhaps there are ghosts. Perhaps not.

If Aeschylus' *The Kindly Ones* takes us into a different world from that of the other two plays, so does Harris's final drama, *Electra and Her Shadow*. By Aeschylus, we are brought into a more rational world, one where reason may prevail, one in which a certain light is let in to the sometimes grimly atavistic language of the preceding plays. By Harris, we are ushered into a modern psychiatric ward: the place where, in our own world, we are brought in the last resort to banish the demons that haunt us. Again comes the dance between the external and internal: it is never quite clear whether we are witnessing hauntings in the outer, visible world, or ones that takes place entirely in the minds of the characters. There is a moment in *The Bough Breaks* when, looking into her brother's face,

Electra says, 'It's like a mirror', and for a while in the third play it seems as if violence will bounce back its image in infinite regression, as if the madness will never end. But Harris's play shows that inner resources can, in some cases, be found to heal deep and seemingly intractable pain, and to dislodge the mechanisms of apparently endless cycles of behaviour.

All translations, versions, or adaptations of works involve a conversation with an earlier writer; an encounter, in this case, across the span of two-and-a-half millennia. Aeschylus' *Oresteia* was itself a conversation with Homer, taking the *Odyssey*'s accounts of Agamemnon's return home and radically expanding and reimagining them. Harris's trilogy *This Restless House* is another iteration of this long conversation between dramatists and poets of different eras, one that sees the fertile stories of the Greeks doing what they have always done: seeding themselves in the minds of writers and then generating new stories for new times.

THIS RESTLESS HOUSE

PART ONE
AGAMEMNON'S RETURN

Characters

Chorus
of old and dishevelled men

Iphigenia

Watchman

Clytemnestra

Ianthe

Electra

Messenger

Agamemnon

Cassandra

Aegisthus

An assortment of hangers-on

Act One

SCENE ONE

A Chorus of old and dishevelled men come on to the stage. They stagger, they limp. Some may even crawl. If they had names they would be things like 'the ancient one', 'the one who can't see', 'hollow face', or 'lost in his own thoughts'.

Once on, they look straight at the audience. They stare at the audience without flinching, brazen. One of them has a slight tic, another occasionally moans.

Chorus
    go on then avert your gaze
    look away
    don't stare at us for too long
    turn your heads gentlewomen
    men hide behind your hands
    you walk past us on the street after all
    you close your curtains
    shut your door
    we've seen you do it
    you bolt the gate and bolt it again
    who can blame you?
    we are the abandoned
    left out in the rain
    yes the given-up on by the gods
    and who wants that to cross their land?

They look around.

    don't worry we are impotent
    we can hardly stand
    we won't chase you
    the most we will do is kind of half a wave

don't get too near though you might catch something
the shake my hand and my arm falls off
the don't mind my leg, it's just a stump
why have the gods left us to this? you ask
did we deserve our witless state?
our pain?
did we offend them?
good question
curse them perhaps?
we aged that's all.
some are blessed, others not it seems
we sit here as a reminder
say your prayers
do what they tell you
for the gods have no mercy
and life can be long

They look out at the audience.

oh, no one's leaving?
there's the door
let me tell you this tale is not for everyone
and it's not going to be funny either
comedy this is not
if you want to laugh try elsewhere we suggest

Pause.

alright, we'll start then
the story starts ten years ago
right here in Greece
a woman called Helen
a married woman
a queen
smiled too sweetly at another man
it's not the smile that mattered
would the gods have minded a smile?
it's a euphemism
screw the euphemism

you don't run off to Troy to 'smile' at someone
she was snatched, Paris took her
no, she was a harlot
a slut, she opened her legs
she defied the rules of marriage, let us say that
offended the gods
and her husband King Menelaus
fucked-off and fearful of the payback from above
he had to act
so he and his brother, our King Agamemnon got together
they raised an army to bring her back
well – there followed a war
a holy war –
you might have heard of it
a war so terrible
you remember the horse?
I actually think, it starts years before that
it starts with a meal that was served to Thyestes,
    that's where it starts
yes the meal of his roasted children, he's right
before then though the house of Atreus was cursed
you have to go right back to the beginning to
    understand the blight on this place
the gods have never been happy
I think it started with a girl
Iphigenia
bless her holy name
you can't start with Iphigenia
why not?
it starts with the eagle
the eagle yes, the day of the sailing
even you agree now?
two armies line up, ready to set sail to get Helen
the two kings at their helm
Menelaus and Agamemnon,
temples visited, prayers said

anxious to set off and bring the beauty home
when overhead, two eagles
soaring
one black one white
fly across, make a great arc in the sky
and everyone remarking
look at that they said
at first they thought it was a blessing from above
oh what luck, two eagles flying over two armies
a sign of the gods' delight
one black one white
and on the right-hand side too
the side of fortune
what a great day, everyone said
victory is written, given from the heavens
this is a holy war indeed blessed from the start
the army were delighted
the wives saying goodbye to their husbands, reassured
traders knowing their workforce would return
smiles all around
but then those birds,
on closer look, those eagles
turned – a bit ugly
not so nice after all
savage in fact
they swooped down and seeing a hare
large with babies
right there with the army and crowd watching
they ripped it without a second's thought
ate it
tossing its body
it makes me scratch to remember
it was a bit revolting truth be told
graphic, you know how these things can be
the babies still quivering
what does it mean, King Agamemnon? the soldiers cried

what does it signify, King Menelaus? asked the army
    wives
if this came from the gods then what is the message?
King Agamemnon couldn't answer
he was as stumped as they were
and, not liking to be silent in front of his people,
he called for the holiest in the city
the high priest and his entourage
the holy man came to the port, looked at the shredded
    hare
chewed his beard
stroked his face
it means victory of some sort, that is certain
a blessing he said
the crowd go crazy
but that's not all, he adds
the gods have given you a coda
a little postscript
you aren't making sense your holiest
King Agamemnon then irritated
the holy man raised his voice
yes, you will take Troy
restore honour to marriage
yes, you will slaughter the men
yes, you will walk over the corpses of those you have
    killed
but –
after
afterwards perhaps –
here is the uncomfortable coda –
the gods see all the death ahead and are not happy
what do you mean holy man?
Agamemnon again
restless
irritated
the gods can't be against us?

no, but there's a cost for this war,
and they want you to feel it
what? they cried, you aren't being clear
the gods aren't being clear came the reply
but I think they need appeasing

Beat.

and that is how he left a worried King
a father
the army ready to depart
let's just go
his first thought
stupid holy man, what does he know of gods and wars?
let's just –
be off
let's just –
get out of here, do the damn thing
we are assured that the gods are on our side
but the weather was not with them
a storm, a hurricane
every time they left the port, they were blown back
it's too dangerous the King was told to leave in this
    weather
the ships were being wrecked on their own rocks
it's the gods cried the naval officers
I told you said the holy man
they need appeasing

Beat.

and so the lonely King –
this is the part you might not like –
the faint-hearted still have a chance to leave
it's a bit, you know, the next bit
you have to understand how it is for men like
    Agamemnon
himself a holy leader
anointed by the heavens themselves
the men already sick from being on the boat, and not

having even left the shore
his brother, miserable and worried for his city
the crowd, bloodthirsty for victory
he took to prayer
he went down on his knees and offered himself
listened
harder
and harder
until
he knew he had to offer something so dear that the
    tears fell as he heard the answer
something so precious –
NO, not that, he shouted out
then be damned, howled the gods right back
I am damned if I do, and damned if I don't he answered
    in a sweat
do what? said his wife
his Queen
Clytemnestra – his only true love
busy with their new-born
do what, precisely?
but he couldn't tell her
how could he even utter the words?
do what? she repeated
but he shook his head and left her alone
do what? she shouted after him. Do what? Do what?
this is where the daughter comes in
this is where, well
well what is there more precious to a father than a
    daughter?
any daughter, but Iphigenia?
bless her holy name
what is there more precious to lose?
Iphigenia was their first born
others came later – Orestes, Electra – but Iphigenia,
even the people who weren't her father had to agree
she was pretty special

a much-loved child, adored by her parents
not spoiled but –
tell them about the suitcase
the suitcase kind of breaks my heart, do we have to
     talk about the case?
tell them about the yellow dress then
do we have to fill in the details?
they have imaginations, they can colour it in for
     themselves
but without the stain, without the detail?
what is a story without the pigmentation?
Iphigenia
bless her holy name
just eleven
her body just starting to show the first signs of
     womanhood
Iphigenia
dressed in yellow
cadmium yellow
with a red ribbon
and carrying a little case
close to cornflower blue
into which she had put everything she could think of
     for her father's trip
what does a man need, when he is to become a soldier?
she thought
what is required?
will he know how to be brave out there?
will he be courageous?
he has never fought much before, will he know how
     to fight?
and so she had looked it up
Burdock
came the answer
Burdock for brutality
a little well-pressed and made into a poultice

Burdock for brutality
and Bilberry for bludgery
and so she put them into the case
Foxgloves for fearlessness;
Garlic for endurance, crushed up, and eaten raw.
Mistletoe, to lose all gentle spirit,
Willow to feel unabashed, brazen,
Comfrey to feel no pain.
Dandelion as blood-thickener.
cleanse the spirit with Guelder Rose,
Camphor stored in oil increases strength
Liquorice for courage.
Thyme to clean wounds, Lavender to sleep when you
    need to.
only don't sleep for long, she told him
wake up fresh and start again, you've got might on
    your side but you can't be complacent.
Caraway for cruelty.
Hibiscus, Hawthorn to bring you luck.
Sweet Linden to forget.

*A girl of about eleven and dressed in yellow comes on to
the stage and watches them, unnoticed. She is carrying a
little blue suitcase.*

only there'll be no forgetting she told him. Only of
    the city when it's done. We'll get the news then we'll
    celebrate me and Mummy, and the baby, we'll be
    laughing. You did it, you went and did it. That's
    what we will say. Even the infant will talk. You
    fucking nailed it

Beat.

and the father
in answer
and now convinced
took his girl and embraced her

27

this girl he had cradled so many times through so
    many nights
this child he had so often sung to sleep
he put his big soldier hands around her back
and tight
tighter than he had ever held her before
and get off Dad and what are you doing?
and holding out his knife
tears already in his eyes
but Daddy said the girl
is this a game? You're hurting me
your grip is so hard
no game
he said and
I'm sorry my love
the rain now heavy and running
the gods have made me
what then, she asked seeing the knife
a look of terror in her eye
a scream
panic setting in
realising she was caught
the trap made from her father's hands
let me go
let me go let me go
the blood
already forming on the yellow dress
Daddy she screamed out
with a sound that no child should make
let me go
no child should even hear
the cry of the torture chamber
of the horror unbelieving
the pleading, the clutching
still surely a game
Daddy

but the knife was in her back and not watching how
   she flailed
he put it in and in and in
and again
a frenzy now
a thin line of sweat on his upper lip from all his work
and in and in and in
until she –

Pause.

then lifeless and limp
and covered in blood, he put her on the sand
and he raised his hands to the skies above, and said see
I did it,
I did what you asked
and now can I sail to victory?

*The girl is sitting on the ground with her little blue
suitcase in front of her.*

Iphigenia
a compass? I know you don't need it. A plastic plate
   to eat your dinner off, a woollen hat for the cold
   and a pair of gloves? Don't laugh at me
a knife to slice out the eyes of the enemy. Don't you
   want that?
some hemlock and belladonna for Helen the whore?
you have to think like a savage if you're going
   to win

*She pushes the case in front of her. As if she expects the
other person to take it.*

She feels in her pockets.

Beat.

I haven't got anything else.
I put it altogether. I put it in a case. Won't you take it?

I sewed a little row of hearts on a cloth, you could
    keep it at your breast? And I know stitches are just
    cotton and commonplace, but maybe by some
    charm they'll bring you back safe –

Beat.

    Daddy?

The heavens open. It starts to rain.

    Daddy?

Her dress runs red.

    DADDY?

Chorus
    can we save her?
    she's a ghost
    bless her holy name
    you can't even touch her

Iphigenia
    DADDY?

Chorus
    must we watch it?
    put up your umbrellas, shield yourselves
    I can't see it again
    we've watched it every night for ten years
    no more

Her last scream curdles the blood.

Iphigenia
    DADDY

They put up their umbrellas. The rain comes down hard.

A moment passes.

Then the rain eases. They take their umbrellas down.

The ghost has gone.

Chorus
the mother should have buried her
I agree
properly, she's a martyr
she did bury her
she came down to the sand when she heard what
    he had done
she had her carried from the shore
yes but
not a proper grave
a grave in the garden – tut –
the girl needed a proper grave
oh the mother should have buried but the father was
    alright to slaughter her? It's the mothers fault that
    she can't rest?!
the gods asked it, of course he was right
we saw him anguish, didn't we?
kneel down in prayer?
it was a holy act
not holy enough –
don't even think that, do you want them to curse
    us more?
who's that?
where?
another ghost?
this is the night for them
he has a torch
shush, maybe he won't see us

A Watchman enters. Dressed for the cold.

Watchman
who are those voices? I can hear you

Chorus
just the old sir
the lame
the weird

31

Watchman
I can't see your faces, do I know you?

Chorus
we mean you no harm

The Chorus step forward, the rain has stopped.

Watchman
praise the gods then

Chorus
in all things and all ways

Greeting over, the Watchman looks at them.

Watchman
well help me up
my legs are as bad as yours

Chorus
we can't lift you sir
we are the useless. the forgotten

Watchman
give me a hand I said

Chorus
you see the grass that grows around us

Watchman
what, you can do nothing?

Chorus
we can sit
sometimes we can chew on very softened food
sometimes we lift a very heavy finger to shoo a very
    tired insect

The Watchman manages to get up on to the stage.

Watchman
you need to get your ideas about you then

there's news tonight
look over there

Chorus
where?

Watchman
a light
this isn't the night to sit about complaining about
your crippled legs, how your old teeth ache
this is the night to be leaping, running, shouting
with joy
there's news

Chorus
what news?

Watchman
the best news of all
you see – there? A flare

They all look.

Chorus
I'm not sure where we are looking

Watchman
behind, there – further over

Chorus
I see it
I don't
lend him your eye-thing

Watchman
are you the blind as well as the infirm? Goodness sake
there.

Chorus
I still can't see it
you are looking the wrong way, over there

Watchman
> ten years I've been watching. Ten years up that hill,
> and looking at nothing. Absolutely nothing.
> but tonight
> tonight my useless friends –

Chorus
> and it means?

Watchman
> and it means? And it means? Only the best it could mean
> Troy has fallen
> that's what it means
> it means we did it
> they did it
> merciful are the gods
> ten years it might have taken sure but
> they fucking nailed it
> move out of the way, I need to get to the bell

Chorus
> you are waking the household?

Watchman
> yes

Chorus
> are you sure?
> the royal household?

Watchman
> the Queen will want to want to wake up
> give me a better reason to wake a queen

Chorus
> it's just
> the Queen
> she needs notice sometimes

Watchman
> what do you mean, notice?

Chorus
 you can't just barge in
 and, well, not so very long ago
 you remember the past?
 things have always been bleak around here, let's
    be honest
 and now this
 good news, blessings?
 it just doesn't sit well
 I agree

Watchman
 wake up, misfits
 shake off whatever place or dream you were in
 you aren't listening
 open your ears, your bloodshot eyes
 see – a fire – like the sun
 that is no omen
 it's a fire lit by a watchman like me
 a final flame in a great chain of flames lit right the
    way across Greece.
 look
 the Greeks have won
 that's what it says
 Agamemnon fucking nailed it
 he fucking nailed it
 and tip of the top
 he's coming home
 Agamemnon's coming home

The Watchman rings the bell for all he's worth.

SCENE TWO

*The late stages of a private party in the palace. Only this
is not a party of celebration, rather the sort of party that
happens too often, with the same hangers-on and the*

35

same host singing the same song as she drinks too much. It has a queer quality, maybe some women dressed as men, old men dressed as women.

Clytemnestra is the host, looking worse for wear and dripping in admirers and adornments. She is standing at a microphone singing a song, karaoke-style.

She gets the tune wrong and has to go back to the start. The song is a lament for someone you once loved. It has a chorus that the people around her join in with, in as much as they can. Some are asleep, some are stoned. No one is sober.

The song describes the feeling of being in love and how the singer thought it might last forever.

There is a kind of harmony and joint endeavour of singing the song through.

The song comes to an end.

Someone shouts out a suggestion – another song. This time about the rain.

Clytemnestra
we sang that yesterday

Partygoer
again

Clytemnestra
alright but you'll have to give me the note

They begin the second song.

A female assistant, Ianthe, comes in and whispers something in Clytemnestra's ear.

The hangers-on carry on singing. Heartily now.

Clytemnestra has stopped.

She grabs Ianthe; she needs to hear what she said again.

Ianthe whispers again.

*The people around her haven't noticed that Clytemnestra
has stopped singing.*

She wants them all to stop. Now.

She rips out the microphone.

Clytemnestra
time to go home.

There is general grumbling – what about the song. etc.

She starts to shove and pull at the sleeping.

party's over – wake up
didn't you hear me?
no, I'm not joking – sudden apologies but I mean it,
   yes go home

Sleeping Person
now wait a second –

Clytemnestra
the door is right there, if you have trouble finding it
someone help them get up –!

She pushes at someone else, pours water on another.

She is scary when she is like this.

why haven't you all disappeared already? I made it
   clear haven't I? The words did come out of my
   mouth? Get out of here – the party is over

They are surprised at the quick change in her.

don't look at me like that. It's my house isn't it? My
   palace. I'll send for you, we'll sing again – but now.
   Go. Go go. Could I have a glass of water? Please.
   Someone a glass of water. No not you, you can run.
   Disappear.

I don't want to be rude, but –
and my daughter. Someone get my daughter here,
    wake her if you need to.
and some coffee perhaps.
strong coffee. Is it too much to ask?

They have all picked themselves and gone.

She is alone.

She kicks at the debris. As she kicks, one of the electric instruments gives some feedback. She thumps at it, then crumples a bit.

She finds a last partygoer crumpled in among the drums.

She shoos them off.

Then alone again – she looks up to the heavens.

fucking hell.
this? Really?

She feels very alone for a second surrounded by the debris of the party.

She picks up an abandoned wine glass. Throws the dregs down her throat.

A girl appears through the open door, the girl is wearing a yellow dress. Close to cadmium yellow.

don't judge me
don't look at me like that.
I'll sober up. I always do.
you know I do
I can't actually deal with you right now, do you have
    to come now. This hour, was this the exact one
    to come?

Girl
    Mummy?

Clytemnestra

don't touch me, I can't think when you are – stay
    further back or even better turn around and go back
    to where you came from
hell fiend
freak of nature –

Girl

Mummy

Clytemnestra

how can you say that word – you're nothing, you're –
    dust, you're a shadow

Girl

it's Electra

*Electra, Iphigenia's sister, looks identical to the girl we
saw at the start.*

Clytemnestra

Electra?
you aren't Electra, Electra is a baby, Electra is . . .
oh God.
Electra? I'm sorry.
oh my baby. I'm not thinking, this news, I –

Electra

did they win?

Clytemnestra

did who win?

Electra

Daddy's army

Clytemnestra

yes Daddy's army won

Electra

and Daddy?

Clytemnestra
yes and Daddy too

Electra
the whole war, he won it?

Clytemnestra
that's right, my baby girl

Electra
isn't that good?

Clytemnestra
it's good, yes. It's very good

She laughs.

it's fantastic. The best. It's not all that good for the
  Trojans, truthfully, but for us. Yes. It couldn't be
  better. They won't be back for a while, but when
  they do – there'll be dancing in the square. It will
  be like a party, the biggest party you've ever seen –
who told you to put this dress on by the way?

Electra
you did

Clytemnestra
I did? This one?

Electra
you said if it was ever good news I had to wear this
  dress

Clytemnestra
maybe this dress is for another day, maybe this dress
  should wait for the grand arrival, for when they get
  here, even though it looks so good on you, too good
  maybe it looks. I think you should take it off, don't
  get it dirty, don't stand in the rain

She holds her tight.

don't stand in the rain

Electra

    Mummy?

Clytemnestra

    never stand in the rain in this dress
    do you hear me?

Electra

    what's wrong?

A second girl, Iphigenia, comes in through the door. She is wearing the same dress. Clean now, no blood.

Clytemnestra notices her, stiffens slightly perhaps, but does nothing.

Clytemnestra

    today is going to be busy that is all. We need to clear
    up, get rid of all this crap. I should have cleaned up
    years ago, and now – you can help or stay with
    your toys. Smile at anyone, everyone. Say you are
    delighted, if anyone asks you. You're delighted, you
    can't wait to see your father. That is all you need
    to say. He fucking nailed it, you can say that if
    you like.

Clytemnestra throws another dreg-end of wine down her throat.

Iphigenia might pick up one of the musical instruments that has been left by the party makers.

    he fucking nailed it

Iphigenia starts to pluck.

Clytemnestra stiffens, made uncomfortable by her presence.

Electra

    I don't like it

Clytemnestra

    you don't like what?

Electra
everything will be different, strange

Clytemnestra
better maybe
don't worry they won't be back for a little while –

Electra
I never met him

Clytemnestra
you did, you just don't remember. You were a baby

Electra
he's a soldier

Clytemnestra
not here, here he is just a man
and a leader, of course. A king.

Electra
will I recognise him?

Clytemnestra
yes by his broad arms, just right for picking a girl up
and holding her tight. Blue eyes that light up when
you smile at them, clean-shaven, or he was maybe
now he has a beard. Brown hair, probably greyed a
little in ten years but soft to cuddle into. Maybe
some really impressive battle scars to tell your
friends about.

Electra
what if I don't like him?

Clytemnestra
you'll love him.
that's the problem. You'll absolutely love him

The other girl strums on the instruments again.

now we need to get on, I need to –

I don't even know what I need to do. We'll stick
    together you and me
this palace used to be gleaming, a jewel they called it

Ianthe comes in again.

Ianthe
madam, there's some women outside asking for you

Clytemnestra
already?

Ianthe
what should I say to them?

Clytemnestra
say that they can't speak to the Queen until later
could I have some clothes, I did ask

Ianthe
they're asking for confirmation, whether it's true

Clytemnestra
I need coffee, is someone bringing me some coffee –

Ianthe
they want to know when the men will come back

Clytemnestra
I understand what they want, and they'll get it but
    even you wouldn't want me to go out to them like
    this? How can I confirm it? I have only heard the
    same rumour as them

Ianthe
they may break through the gates

Clytemnestra
take Electra to the kitchen. Don't let anyone see her
    unless I am there. The women can wait, they have
    waited for ten years so another ten minutes – and
    we need to clean up, get rid of all this junk. It's

alright sweetheart, it's going to be okay. In essence
it's a brilliant day. A day for a party. Please don't
worry –

The girl strums on the musical instrument again.

wait. Have you got anything for pain? I've got a
terrible headache

Ianthe looks through her bag.

She hands over a little box.

Ianthe
you're supposed to take two

Clytemnestra
I'll take four

*Clytemnestra takes some pinches of the substance and
snorts.*

Ianthe
four should cure any headache

Clytemnestra
then I'll take eight

She takes some more.

Ianthe passes her something to wipe her nose.

you would think ten years, the girl and I would have
had a little time to prepare ourselves, you would
think that as I have spent most of the last ten years
imagining this I would know what I am doing, what
I should say but . . .

The girl strums again.

it's just this head.
I can deal with the women, the people, once I am
dressed I can deal with anything. We'll get the public
bit over, then in private –

44

Ianthe
  it's going to take some time to get used to each other

Clytemnestra
  I can't even think about it

Ianthe
  one day at a time

Clytemnestra
  I haven't been outside for years, and then today
  you've seen everything you know exactly what I've
      become. I can't go out in front of anyone

Ianthe
  take another

Clytemnestra
  I need some time, stall them
  at least let me put on my face –

A bell starts to ring.

  what have I become?

Ianthe
  the victory bell

Clytemnestra
  maybe that will keep them happy for a while?
  tell them their gods have looked kindly, I don't care

Ianthe
  shall I tell them the Queen will be with them shortly?

Clytemnestra
  not shortly, when I'm ready
  when will that be? Never
  when I'm – do you think I'll ever be clear headed again?
  properly sober?

Ianthe
  of course you will

Ianthe turns to Electra and takes her hand.

    come on, sweetheart

Ianthe and Electra leave.

Clytemnestra starts to get ready. She drinks some coffee. She takes some of the party stuff off. She might wipe her face.

The other girl strums again.

Clytemnestra
    don't do that. Will you stop doing that?
    are you trying to crack my head into pieces?

The girl plays again.

    I don't know what you want from me. Whatever you
        think I can do, I can't. I can't even. It's impossible.
        The thought of it, I – do I look like someone that
        can do it? Weak, forceless, I'm feeble. I'm a tiny
        little flea, a mouse. A worm. I'm nothing, I might
        have given birth to you but what have I done since?
    I could lock the doors, not let him in.
    never see him again. Wouldn't that be enough?
    he should have died on the battlefield, that's what
        should have happened. He should have been snared,
        enflamed, run through, if there was justice –

The girl comes and takes the face wipe. She wipes her mother's face.

She uses her own spit.

    I can't do it

The girl starts to go.

    I am spineless, a spent force. Any power I had I lost.
    I'll muck it up, I'll get it wrong. Don't leave me
    don't put the thought there then disappear again.

46

Oi don't do that. Come back. You planted it there,
   so, what, am I just be left with this? Iphigenia, I'm
   talking to you!

She looks around.

The wind blows the curtains at the window.

SCENE THREE

*The square outside the palace. A large screen has been
put up, and there are banners and decorations. Ianthe has
a large brush and is brushing the square. Someone else is
scrubbing the walls.*

The Chorus come on and watch her.

Chorus
   I don't like it
   what?
   this clean thing,
   look the graffiti's disappeared
   now that's a shame
   it used to say fuck the Trojans, take one up the arse
   it was the ten-foot penis aimed at Troy I liked
   and the words 'Praise Be' right underneath
   where are we supposed to sit?
   yes, the chairs have gone –
   and the moss
   we've sat here for all these years, don't tell me we have
      to find somewhere else?
   rampant dishonesty, that's what I call it
   sterility
   papering over the cracks
   oi bring back the pigeons
   the moss
   the penises!

47

The Watchman comes on.

He is feeling merry.

Watchman
well that was predictable

Chorus
what do you mean?

Watchman
everyone working hard to do a clean-up job and you
missing the shit

Chorus
we were used to it

Watchman
I've been ten years up a hill
let me tell you, this place is brilliant
plus I just got a new job

Chorus
what job?

Watchman
standing at the metal barriers
keeping the crowds out

Chorus
congratulations

Watchman
when the King gets back, there'll be thousands coming
here.

Chorus
they'll be waiting to greet their own

Watchman
that too
but this country has gone to the dogs, now with this –

48

could be the boost we all need.
plus anything beats staring at the sky

Chorus
something isn't right though, is it?

Watchman
here we go

Chorus
does nobody else feel it?

Watchman
it's good news today, we could try to be elated

Chorus
do you think this house, after so much trouble is about
    to settle down?

Watchman
the gods have blessed us, what is wrong with you?
you could try saying thanks
thanks up there, we appreciate it
and the palace by the way, is going to look great

Chorus
the flies then

Watchman
what about the flies?

Chorus
well where have they gone?

Watchman
you are complaining the flies have gone now?

Chorus
the pigeon shit has been removed,
they have nothing to feed off
they're pressed against the windows, buzzing to get
    inside.

Watchman
> honestly, you realise what you are saying?
> the gods just blessed this city
> bloody won us the war
> they need us to notice, say thank you
> so notice

He gets out a bottle.

> thanks up there.
> and praise be

He reluctantly shares his drink with the Chorus.

Chorus
> I wonder what they they'll be drinking over there

Watchman
> where?

Chorus
> Troy

Watchman
> you are like a widow at a wedding, must you always
> be so fucking morose?

Chorus
> well said
> they'll all be dead, the people of Troy

Watchman
> the women?

Chorus
> they'll be dead too, raped until they keeled over

Watchman
> the children then

Chorus
> pretty much dead as well
> shut him up
> they have the same gods don't they?

Watchman
for heaven's sake

Chorus
don't say that
they are heathens
I mean just for a moment, think of the logic
the gods smile on us, but they frowned on them?

Watchman
they started it

Chorus
did the children start it?

Watchman
Paris started it
if you want to live a good life, don't live under a stupid
leader. Someone should write that in stone and put
it up in temple square. Or more – if you want to be
a good leader, then keep it in your trousers.
Someone should have said that to Paris. Helen's not
for you, sunshine, she's married, get over it. What
was he expecting? You can't spit at the gods and
expect a good outcome

Chorus
so they deserved it?

Watchman
absolutely. Death to the lot of them.
and long may the heavens smile on us.
cheers

They drink.

oi sour chops, come over here

Ianthe
don't call me that

Watchman
come and have a drink with us –

Ianthe
what are you even doing here, how did you get in?

Watchman
I've got a job

Ianthe
here?

Watchman
security

Ianthe
well you go and do it then

Watchman
I'm celebrating

Ianthe
are you crazy?

Watchman
just a little tipple

Ianthe
you have to move on, this place has all got to be
    spruced up
and this lot, out

Watchman
they're my friends

Ianthe
don't be absurd

Watchman
why not?

Ianthe
they're ugly, grotesque

Watchman
that's a bit strong –

Chorus
we can actually hear you

Ianthe
revolting
and no one is to be here without a permit whatever
you smell like

The Watchman laughs.

Watchman
you don't usually mind

Ianthe
will you get off my case and do what you're told?

Watchman
listen sweetheart

Ianthe
don't sweetheart me

Watchman
alright

Ianthe
alright

The Watchman goes off.

Watchman
I'll see you later then

Ianthe
don't count on it

Watchman
that's what you always say

Ianthe looks the way he went. Irritated.

Chorus
you can't move us on
we've been here so long have rights

Ianthe
what rights?

Chorus
by every right,

Ianthe
do you want me to go and call for some reinforcements?

Chorus
from who?

Ianthe
security

Chorus
what that guy there?

Ianthe
I'll get you kicked off, and I'll get you thrown in
    the river
and I'll make sure your legs are broken so you can't
    swim to the bank

Clytemnestra
let them stay

Clytemnestra has appeared from one of the doors.

Ianthe
madam?

Clytemnestra
let them stay
they're right, they have been here for years and today –

Ianthe
are you sure?

Clytemnestra
yes, go, I know you are busy.

Ianthe
the crowds are building up, we aren't prepared for this

Clytemnestra
no one was prepared for this
if anyone had been prepared for this –
the war was unwinnable, that's what we were told

Ianthe
praise be to the gods

Clytemnestra
of course

Ianthe moves on with the brush.

Clytemnestra almost squints at the light. She puts on some sunglasses.

how long does it take a ship to get back to Greece do
    you think?
and don't say it depends on the weather.
two days? Three

Chorus
not sure

Clytemnestra
the women are all asking
I don't have an answer for them

Chorus
we . . .

Clytemnestra
tell me I have days yet.
sometimes I look out of the window and I can hear
    you down here, muttering away
and I wish I could crawl in amongst you, put on an old
    coat that smells of drink and urine and hide

55

could I hide for a while?
there in the midst of you
where not even ghosts can reach me?
just there where I could drink from a bottle –

She reaches for the bottle.

and one of you could take my place?

Chorus
madam?

Clytemnestra
why not? It's got to be worth a try hasn't it? I could
    just – sink, sink in my last moments –

The noise of fighting disturbs them. A brawl.

*The Watchman is caught up trying to push the Messenger
off.*

Messenger
where's the Queen?

Ianthe
you're supposed to be at the barriers

Watchman
I tried to stop him

Messenger
I have a delivery for her
I was told to bring it in person

Ianthe
what delivery?

The Messenger gets out a dress.

Clytemnestra
what the hell?

Messenger
made with silk from Troy

Clytemnestra stands up.

    the King wanted you to have something
    to say he hasn't stopped thinking about you for
      a second

Clytemnestra doesn't say anything.

The Messenger hands her the dress.

    I think he picked it himself

Clytemnestra
    it has a split up the side
    and is low-cut

She doesn't take the dress.

Messenger
    would you like to take it?

Clytemnestra
    wasn't he fighting a war not thinking about me?

Messenger
    the dress was sent in love

Clytemnestra
    lust

Messenger
    I'm just saying –

Clytemnestra
    that I should take it, because he sent it?
    is that what you are saying?
    put it on, look sexy when he arrives?

Beat.

Ianthe sees the awkwardness and takes the dress.

Ianthe
    I'll see it is hung up in the wardrobe

Messenger
thank you

Ianthe
that's quite alright. It's beautiful

Messenger
it's made of silk

Ianthe
I can see that

The Messenger still stands there.

Clytemnestra
is there something else?

Messenger
I think he was hoping for something in reply

Clytemnestra
?

Ianthe
he wants her to say something?

Messenger
I think so yes
has she got something to say to her husband?

Ianthe looks at the Queen.

The Queen looks at the Messenger.

Clytemnestra
no. Not really.

Messenger
nothing?

Beat.

Ianthe
madam, if I might just –

58

Ianthe turns to Clytemnestra to speak quietly.

Clytemnestra
what is this?

Ianthe
can we just think for a second?

Clytemnestra
a fucking dress, split up the side?

Ianthe
you need to say something

Clytemnestra
what the fuck should I say?

Ianthe
the man is a hero
after all this blood, they need some joy. The King and
Queen reunited after so long. It's a perfect story –

Clytemnestra
and me?

Ianthe
just say something, you're pleased or –

Messenger
is there a problem?

Ianthe
no problem.

Messenger
it is almost as if she has no joy at this news

Chorus
of course she feels joy,
how could she not?

Messenger
so why keep him waiting –

Clytemnestra takes a deep breath. She starts to speak. She stops.

Chorus
you can say something can't you?

Ianthe
it doesn't have to be much

There is another wait while Clytemnestra forms the words.

Clytemnestra
just . . .

Chorus
yes?

Beat.

Clytemnestra
just come home sweetheart

Everyone claps and music starts to play.

just come home

The stage erupts into a celebration, balloons, dancing, musicians playing. The slogan 'Just Come Home Sweetheart' is put up on a large banner that crosses the palace. It's that crazy, devil-may-care sort of partying after a long war. It feels like a mardi gras, a fete, a honky-tonk parade.

In amongst the band, a woman takes the microphone and sings a song: 'To my sweetheart, just come home'.

Act Two

The next evening. On top of a hill outside the city.

Two lovers are in a clinch. Then one pushes the other off.

It's the Watchman and Ianthe.

Watchman
would you give me a minute?

Ianthe
you've had a minute

Watchman
I don't know where you get your energy

Ianthe
we haven't got long –

Watchman
just a second

Ianthe
I've got to be back

Watchman
it's not natural

Ianthe
the most natural thing there is, but quickly

Watchman
no not that, not the act, the progression
we go from bam to ahh, and back to bam

Ianthe
what is wrong with that?

Watchman
    no delineation. No pause
    no moment to say that was one, and now this is
        the other

Ianthe
    are you joking?

Watchman
    will you budge off –

Ianthe
    seriously?

Watchman
    I just need a second

Ianthe
    why?

Watchman
    men
    sometimes we need –

Ianthe
    oh I see

Watchman
    just a second or two
    if we could wait a minute

Ianthe
    yes of course but . . .
    how long do you think?

Watchman
    a couple of minutes, that's all

Beat.

Ianthe
    only I'll have to get back to the Queen quite soon

Watchman
what about tomorrow?

Ianthe
will it take that long?

Watchman
no I just meant –

Ianthe
be different tomorrow anyway, no sex tomorrow

Watchman
what?

Ianthe
there'll be the old rules back
we won't just be able to meet on the top of a hill

Watchman
we'll always be able to meet at the top of a hill

Ianthe
you watch. The King comes back and it will all change
men can't do this, women can't do that
the mighty gods will be offended if you so much as
    sneeze outside marriage

Watchman
it's always been like that

Ianthe
the Queen didn't care though did she? We've done
    what we wanted

Watchman
is this supposed to be helping?

Ianthe
I'm just saying tonight might be our last night so
    would you fucking hurry up

Watchman
I'm trying my best

Ianthe
keep trying

Beat.

Watchman
I'll marry you then
if we can't meet on a hill

Ianthe
fuck off.

Watchman
why not?

Ianthe
I have to stay with the Queen, you know that

Watchman
if you want to, we could just go somewhere

Ianthe
what, leave her?

Watchman
doesn't sound like you want to stay

Ianthe
it will all be shit, that's all I am saying
and it starts here
you get the wilts and everything goes phut

Watchman
you know how to get someone in the mood

He straightens his hair. Puts his glasses back on.

bloody hell

Ianthe
yeah well, my mood changed

Watchman
  I think I noticed

Ianthe
  it's cold anyway. My back hurts

Watchman
  really?

Ianthe
  yes really

She gets up and goes off.

She comes back and kisses him.

Ianthe
  I'll find you tomorrow yeah

Watchman
  I mean it, I'll marry you

She leaves him on the hill.

He speaks to himself, alone.

  fucking hell

He looks down.

  oh now you spring into action?
  what timing you have

A man comes in.

Agamemnon, the King.

Agamemnon
  who said that?
  is there someone there?
  damn you, I don't have a torch

Watchman
  just a watchman sir

Agamemnon
then stand up

The Watchman stands up.

Agamemnon
I thought I heard a curse

Watchman
no just me speaking to myself
praise the gods sir

Agamemnon
in all things and in all ways

Agamemnon holds out a lantern.

I thought this hill was out of bounds, but it seems
busy this evening

Watchman
it has a reputation

Agamemnon
this near the palace?
it used to be holy
there was a shrine right here

Watchman
I don't know about a shrine sir

Agamemnon
I haven't been here for a while
tell me how is this city?
the Queen is she well?

Watchman
you are asking me about the Queen?

Agamemnon
yes

Watchman
she is fine, I think

Agamemnon
there's never any word about her
does she govern well?

Watchman
adequately

Agamemnon
and the people, do they love her?

Watchman
as people can

Beat.

Agamemnon
you are right, you're loyal,
you don't know me, why should you answer questions
about the Queen
praise be to the gods

Watchman
in all things and in all ways

Agamemnon
you're good man, I can see that.
when I'm in a position I'll give you a job

Watchman
what position is that sir?

Agamemnon
the highest position I'm hoping, by the Queen's side

Watchman
you shouldn't joke sir
the King will be back tomorrow, he won't like word
of that

Agamemnon
indeed he won't

Watchman
mind you the Queen hasn't forgotten what he did, it's said she won't open the door to him tomorrow

Agamemnon
is that so?

Watchman
it's said she . . .

He stops.

Agamemnon
why have you stopped?

Watchman
it's rumour only, sir

Agamemnon
keep it as rumour then

Beat.

Watchman
praise be to the gods

Agamemnon
in all things and all ways

The Watchman bows a little and makes to go.

Watchman
shit

Agamemnon
don't run away
be the first to greet me at least

Watchman
how can I greet you? You're the King

Agamemnon
welcome me as a friend then

They greet each other.

    you're the first man I have met
    surely you can be warmer than that?

Watchman
    welcome back

Agamemnon
    what were you going to say about the Queen?

Watchman
    the gods are on your side I heard
    ten years and unscathed –
    what can be worse than what you've already faced?

Agamemnon
    will I need luck?

Watchman
    we all need luck.

The Watchman leaves.

Agamemnon is left on the hill, waiting for his wife.

He stamps once or twice. Blows on his hands.

Looks around, still no sign.

Looks up to the skies.

Agamemnon
    don't let me down, I've come this far –

He closes his eyes, speaks to the skies.

    if you need me to fast, to promise a new temple –
    get down on my knees

Clytemnestra comes in.

She stands quite far away from him.

She has a torch with her, which she puts down.

69

Agamemnon gets up from his knees.

They look at each other for a second before they speak.

Agamemnon
thank you

Clytemnestra
you don't need to thank me

Agamemnon
thank you for coming

Clytemnestra
you're my husband, of course I would come

Agamemnon
you didn't need to, I was careful with my wording
you were on no account to feel obliged

Clytemnestra
I was interested

Agamemnon
interested?

Clytemnestra
well we'll meet of course tomorrow
the crowds will be there when we meet but

Agamemnon
you are so beautiful

Clytemnestra
don't

Beat.

are you injured?

Agamemnon
slightly
some old injuries
I was impaled once, here

recovered
thought I might lose a leg at another moment
recovered
my skull was crushed almost totally on one side
recovered
toes frozen from frostbite, recovered
this wrist snapped in two places, recovered
shall I go on?

Clytemnestra
the point is made

Agamemnon
dozens of injuries mostly recovered

Clytemnestra
the gods were on your side then

Agamemnon
the gods yes

Beat.

I know there is a lot to say
I know that
and I know that ten years weren't long enough to try
    to find the words. I doubt ten lifetimes would be
    long enough
I also know that every person in this country thinks
    I am a hero, and yet –
we will talk if you want it
we can start at the beginning or pick up at the end
I will do whatever you want
but only if you want
that's what I wanted to say
tomorrow of course the crowds expect a great
    reunion

Clytemnestra
the dress?

Agamemnon
  was for the crowd
  stupid maybe
  if it was foolish then I'm sorry –
  if you didn't like it –

Beat.

  I have something I want to ask
  a question
  a statement of intent
  the country may expect it, but –
  if you want I won't turn up at the palace tomorrow
  if you want, I will steer my ship and find somewhere
    else to go
  I won't bother you again
  if you want
  you and I never have to see each other again

Clytemnestra
  if I want?

Agamemnon
  yes
  or, if you don't want the fuss, we live our lives in
    public after all, if you would rather I arrived at the
    palace as planned, and we went through the
    motions of greeting, of loving devotion, but once
    inside, we build a wall between your side of the
    palace and mine and I will never cross that line,
    or even speak to you unless invited. I can do that
  all of that, and more
  you can fashion it yourself, as you like
  but if there is anything –
  if there is a tiny place where you think you can love me
  or understand at least what I had to do
  then please let me know of it
  a word would do, I am not asking for a kiss
  just a simple word of kindness to me

Beat.

> everything will be on your terms, we will go as slow
> as you like

Beat.

> I know it is too much too ask
> I know I presume

Clytemnestra
> what is this word to be?

Agamemnon
> anything
> anything spoken softly
> a gesture
> I don't expect you to be able to answer straight away

Clytemnestra
> I can answer

Agamemnon
> don't be too hasty, take your time

Clytemnestra
> you've spent ten years planning what you wanted
>   to say to me
> do you not think that I would have spent the same
>   length of time planning what I wanted to say to
>   you?

She pauses.

> and yet here now with you in front of me –
> you always confused me
> even when we were teenagers. I would think one thing
>   then when you were there
> the softness is easy
> it seems
> now in this moment

I would only have to half close my mind and
look at you broken and desperate I could take you in
    my arms
of course I could, love like we had doesn't die
but this other flame
this vengeful spirit
this other voice that leads me on
he killed our daughter
he killed our daughter
he killed our daughter

Agamemnon
hush

Clytemnestra
it screams in my ear
how do I quench that?

Agamemnon
with time perhaps?

Clytemnestra
with time?

Agamemnon
perhaps?

Clytemnestra
she was our child, Agamemnon
she was our baby, put here so we could raise her

Agamemnon
the gods

Clytemnestra
don't talk to me about the gods

Agamemnon
the boats then
the wind

74

Clytemnestra
so here we get into it

Agamemnon
only if you want.
only if you want
whatever you want.
okay
okay

Beat.

maybe we shouldn't talk about this now
this wasn't how it was supposed to go

Clytemnestra
did you expect me not to say these things?

Agamemnon
I just wanted to see you
of course you must say them
of course you must say it all
and whatever you say won't be things I haven't already
    thought.
perhaps it's of no consolation or consequence to you,
    but these last ten years I have felt I was drowning
    sometimes
tortured with grief and guilt
the memory of her clutching at me
her eyes pleading
there has been a prison for me, I'll call it hell
do you think I wanted to kill her?
I loved that girl
I loved her like I had never loved before, do you think
    I let myself off?
my Iphigenia, murdered so cruelly, and these my hands
how could I have done it?
I imprisoned myself in my own misery
yes a jail term I served

Clytemnestra
then why do you come to me?

Agamemnon
because it was the gods
because the gods asked of me what was most difficult
    to give and so I had to give it, I had no choice

Clytemnestra
that's the difference between us, I would have gone
    against the gods. Damned myself. I would have been
    ripped from the earth rather than have hurt her.

Agamemnon
I was about to kill the children of others?
I was about to kill and torture a whole town
the gods are just
I had to understand what I was ripping from the world
I had to know, what it means to take a child from a
    family

Clytemnestra
and Iphigenia?
what did she learn?
which 'just' god was looking out for her?

Beat.

why have you come to me, Agamemnon?
like this?
what do you expect from me really?

Agamemnon
some peace
you are the only person who can forgive me

Clytemnestra
you don't even follow your own argument
the gods demanded it, so you are free
innocent

76

Agamemnon
  but not in your eyes

Clytemnestra
  my eyes don't matter

Agamemnon
  they do to me

Beat.

  forgive me?

Beat.

Clytemnestra
  forgive you?
  you said yourself, you don't need forgiving

Agamemnon
  understand me then. Or at least give me some hope
    that one day you might. That if I come home you
    won't punish me with cold words and spite instead
    of love

Clytemnestra
  you want me to love you?

Agamemnon
  I know I ask too much
  I can see the answer in your face
  I'm sorry
  I won't trouble you any more

Beat.

  we will disappoint the crowd, but so what?

Clytemnestra
  the fucking crowd

Agamemnon
  the thousands that have travelled

Clytemnestra
does it matter? What does any of that matter?

Agamemnon
you're right of course

Clytemnestra
they'll hate you

Agamemnon
so be it

Clytemnestra
you always rush me
you always move things too fast

Beat.

Agamemnon
that I loved that little girl can't be in doubt?
right or wrong about the gods, and what they asked,
    but see that I have suffered ten years with the
    memory,
that I will never be free, you can see that surely?

Clytemnestra
I don't know what I see

Agamemnon
you are the only other person that loved her as I do.
can there be no softness between us?
no gentle memories?

Beat.

Clytemnestra
I am out of practice at soft words
I find myself –
you ask for something hard to give
softness? Fuck the softness
softness yes, soft would be lovely

78

to share our grief
to lie here with you, to feel your arms around me
I missed you
I missed you a lot, not as much as I missed her but –
two deaths I felt that day

Agamemnon
I'm not dead

Clytemnestra
but to let you back?
I have been really crazy, these thoughts I have had
put your arms around me – no, don't
I don't know which word to choose, I can see you
   need something but

Agamemnon
any
any word

Beat.

Clytemnestra breathes hard. Confused and upset.

Clytemnestra
don't come near me

Agamemnon
then stop me

He has come over to her.

Clytemnestra
this is not going to be easy. There will be times when
   we will shout and scream and that our child will
   once again come between us, but
I have missed you.
missed the old you, and we –
we will not disappoint the crowd
you loved her yes, I can see that now
I knew it then –

79

Agamemnon
I have lived as a penitent

Clytemnestra
yes perhaps that's a start

Agamemnon
what is the word?

Clytemnestra
the word is
something – neutral
the word is forward-looking but not promising anything
tomorrow.
I can see you tomorrow
you don't have to steer your ship away and live by
    yourself.
your home is here.
they'll be no wall between us
or none of my building
tomorrow
that's my word

*He breathes out, like he has been holding his breath for
a long time.*

He almost breaks down.

Agamemnon
tomorrow?

Clytemnestra
tomorrow

Agamemnon
I love you

Clytemnestra
don't move too fast

Agamemnon
sorry

I didn't say that
I realise, too much –
I just asked for a word, I know
of course, slowly, I said slowly

Clytemnestra
these things will take time
healing like this –

Agamemnon
the rest of our lives
a millennia, as long as you want
all of eternity whatever
thank you
thank you

He takes her hand.

She takes his other one as well.

we had something strong once. Didn't we?
we didn't imagine it?

Clytemnestra
of course we didn't

He kisses her.

I found it so hard to hate you
it drove me mad

Agamemnon
don't then

He kisses again.

Clytemnestra
tell me how much you have suffered –

Agamemnon
every day
always
there was nothing for me out there but my own torment

He kisses her again, she kisses him back.

Clytemnestra
you always make me melt, how do you do that?

Agamemnon
I adore you that's why.
I adore you like no one ever adored anyone

They kiss again.

He has his arms around her.

Another kiss.

She relaxes into him, says fondly:

Clytemnestra
what's that?
around your wrist

Agamemnon
this?
just a keepsake
nothing
someone gave it to me

Clytemnestra
someone gave it to you?

Agamemnon
for luck

Clytemnestra
oh.
who?

Agamemnon
I forget now
one of the men

Clytemnestra
the men made that?

Agamemnon
perhaps one of their wives –
I should ask them

Clytemnestra
which man would give his king something like that?

Agamemnon
a woman then perhaps, it's unimportant

Clytemnestra
a woman?

Agamemnon
there were women in Troy –

Clytemnestra
of course there were –

Agamemnon
we were ten years fighting

Clytemnestra
you were ten years punished by your own thoughts
ten years in your own prison
a kind of hell you called it

Agamemnon
of course yes it was
I don't know why I wear it
it's been so long on my wrist I don't know who put
it there

Clytemnestra
may I have it?

Beat.

may I have it?

Agamemnon
I don't know, these last ten years

Clytemnestra
okay

Agamemnon
it's just always been on my wrist

Clytemnestra
I see
you are fond of it?

Agamemnon
hardly
no, if you want

Clytemnestra
keep it there.

Agamemnon
you understand?

Clytemnestra
of course I do.

Agamemnon
and now I feel the curtain is back up between us

Clytemnestra
no curtain
we have terrain to overcome that is all
some places to navigate
you are a man of course you would need a hole to fuck

Agamemnon
so crude
must you be so crude

Clytemnestra
I'm sorry
a slip

Agamemnon
here you might as well have it
I have all the luck I need

84

Clytemnestra
no leave it where it is
it suits you after all.

Agamemnon
don't be –

Clytemnestra
I'm not

The moment is over, they can't get it back.

Beat.

just when you said you suffered –

Agamemnon
I did suffer

Beat.

I'll leave you now
and see you tomorrow

Clytemnestra
yes

Agamemnon
please, love, don't do this

Clytemnestra
what have I done?
I understand you are man

Agamemnon
yes we are different to what we were
but we can be together, can't we?
tomorrow

Clytemnestra
that word again.
tomorrow

Agamemnon
slowly, slowly we will heal.
I promise

Agamemnon goes.

Clytemnestra is left alone.

She looks around.

Clytemnestra
leave me, ghost
let me make up my own mind
easy for the beetles they have poison already in their
   soul but . . .
I am not a poisonous creature
I always said if I could just stay upright around that
   man, do I need some herbs or
don't confuse me, it isn't fair
I don't know who or what I should be
I don't know what that was

A young woman comes in. This is Cassandra.

Frail, pretty, intelligent.

Also, poorly sighted: she can hardly see.

Cassandra
the willow grows further back
it likes to be near a river, they say it brings decisiveness

Clytemnestra
I didn't ask for help

Cassandra
I heard you calling
so I came

Clytemnestra
what are you, a witch?

Cassandra
    if by that you mean one who can see what others can't
        then yes
    a witch

Clytemnestra
    a weasel a rabbit a transformation?

Cassandra
    no just a woman

Clytemnestra
    I don't believe in gods, if this is some trick

Cassandra
    I'm no god

Clytemnestra
    another ghost?

Cassandra
    definitely not
    see, blood and gristle

Clytemnestra
    you came when I called?

Cassandra
    I was nearby

Clytemnestra
    where is this willow then?

Cassandra
    back there
    by the stream
    I could take you there
    but cudweed is beneath your feet

Clytemnestra looks down.

    they say its roots feed on the sap of the earth
    eat it, and certainty will grow within you

87

Clytemnestra
raw?

Cassandra
if you want
some boil it up and make a tea

Clytemnestra pulls up some and eats it.

and winter sorrel –

Clytemnestra
winter sorrel?

Cassandra
is just over there
chew on the leaves for a clear mind, to overrule the
heart

Clytemnestra
will it work?

Cassandra
be careful that you don't eat too much
it's a difficult thing to reverse
and hibiscus perhaps for determination?
I'll pick you some
you have to be careful, the little thorns. I have some
scissors

Clytemnestra
who are you?

Cassandra
my name is unimportant
I was picking some herbs for dinner

Clytemnestra
you look foreign

Cassandra
I come from Troy

Clytemnestra
  oh
  a slave then

Cassandra
  yes

Clytemnestra
  too bad

Cassandra
  but I am slave to the King

Clytemnestra
  to the King?
  I see

Cassandra
  I turn down his bedcovers

Clytemnestra
  I bet you do

Cassandra
  I arrange his pillows

Clytemnestra
  and suck his cock when he can't sleep?

Cassandra
  yes that too
  mainly rock him though when tears take him

Clytemnestra
  why do tears take him?
  he is the King

Cassandra
  he cries for his dead daughter
  all night sometimes

Beat.

Clytemnestra
trapped then, poor you
slave to someone else's misery

Cassandra
better than being trapped to one's own
besides, not trapped so much
he has a kindness which I can feel in him now

Clytemnestra
how handy

Cassandra
he says he will treat me well

Clytemnestra
does he really?

Cassandra
he says his wife will take me into the household and
welcome me like a friend

Clytemnestra
and what do you say?

Cassandra
I say nothing.
I know she will murder us both

Beat.

Clytemnestra
what?
why did you say that?
murder? Don't speak so loud
the Queen is a good woman

Cassandra
that isn't what they say of her
they say she has turned deranged
all these years with no king

they say she has drunk herself into a stupor and
    neglects her living children
they say she has filled her house with vagrants

Clytemnestra
that isn't a queen I recognise
I have heard she is kind

Cassandra
the opposite then
I tried to warn the King I told him he mustn't go in,
    he should turn his ship away
but he said he would come to her in private, judge
    for himself

Clytemnestra
he said that?

Cassandra
so I wrapped a ribbon around his wrist and told him
    to wear it to keep her evil away

Clytemnestra
her evil?

Cassandra
I can feel it
she will slaughter him and there is nothing that can
    be done
no telling him
no warning he will heed
it's already written in the stars

Clytemnestra
there are some that don't believe in these things any
    more
the gods, the stars

Cassandra
fools then

the gods will punish them for that thought
hibiscus here
you still want it don't you?

The Queen is uncertain whether to take it.

why hesitate now?

Cassandra takes the Queen's hand.

She follows the vein up her arm.

She feels at her face.

but this is the hand that will kill me

Clytemnestra
impossible
the Queen alone on this grubby hill?

Cassandra
this face, this the arm that will strike, yes

Clytemnestra
if you say another word

Cassandra
how can I not say it?
murderess
help, anyone, murderess

Clytemnestra fights Cassandra and pins her down.

Clytemnestra
madness, don't say another word

Cassandra
Apollo enough please
save me, this woman will kill me

Clytemnestra
how could I hurt you?

Cassandra
I'll tell everyone, I will shout it

Clytemnestra
    then I will take your tongue
    I will not kill anyone, impossible

Cassandra pushes Clytemnestra off.

Cassandra
    get off me

Clytemnestra hits back.

Cassandra falls.

Clytemnestra takes the pair of scissors.

She holds Cassandra, who struggles.

She gets her head in a headlock.

    you'll never silence me
    Apollo is my protector, my –

Clytemnestra
    I am not the person you think I am
    I am gentle and kind, damn it

Clytemnestra cuts out her tongue.

Cassandra screams and struggles, falls back, bleeding and in pain.

She scrambles to get up, to run.

Clytemnestra lets her go. She takes stock of herself, covered in this woman's blood.

    oh hell
    how did this . . .?
    oh hell
    hurdles I thought I still had to cross, crossed now
        it seems

She sees the little girl Iphigenia watching her.

    there was doubt in me, but now –
    come then spirit

climb on my back
if I am to do it I need you on my back

The ghost of the little girl appears and climbs on her mother's back.

Clytemnestra stands up, strong now.

And ready.

Interval.

Act Three

The Chorus stand outside the palace. The courtyard is covered in wires and gaffer tape. A gazebo is halfway up. There are stepladders, bits of equipment and some stage lights. Its looks like the chaos of a place that isn't quite ready yet.

The Chorus arrive with arms full of purple cloth.

Chorus
    I can't stand still
    I feel like dancing
    don't dance on my toes
    sorry
    I think we are a bit early
    we shouldn't be here yet
    where should we put this?
    she gave us a permit
    oh this is a lucky day
    we can wait can't we
    we won't get in the way
    will you stop hopping about
    here is my hair straight?
    pass me one of those flowers
    what you going to do with it?
    put in my lapel
    you can't do that
    who is to stop me?
    I think you look good
    thank you
    making new men of us
    who knows what we could achieve from now

this could just be the start
did you ever think – all this, and us

The Watchman comes in. He laughs his head off.

Chorus
did we say something funny?

The Watchman continues to laugh.

he's laughing at us, not with us
he wouldn't do that

Watchman
you lot trussed up like peacocks

Chorus
what peacocks?

Watchman
carrying that thing

Chorus
now wait a minute

Watchman
what did you do, smooth your hair?
clean some vomit off your shirt?
I wouldn't call it transformational

Chorus
thanks very much
we are to be part of the ceremony

Watchman
the Queen is mad, what can I say?

Chorus
we're to put these cloths down for the King

Watchman
insane

Chorus
    when she give us the nod

Watchman
    finally at last she has done it
    gone off her rocker

Chorus
    bugger off

Watchman
    well what other explanation is there?

Chorus
    we're her friends

Watchman
    maybe but
    look around, all this
    classy
    expensive
    serious
    a religious blessing
    giving thanks to the gods
    purple cloths
    that's proper
    like the old days
    and you carrying them?

The Chorus look at themselves.

Chorus
    what's wrong with us?

Watchman
    you know what's wrong with you
    you're revolting
    disgusting
    the bits of humankind we would rather not look at
    the Queen could have asked for help from anyone in
        the city

but she chose you
you have got to ask why, haven't you?

Chorus
she is kind

Watchman
is she known for her kindness?

Chorus
she always let us stay here

Watchman
quite then it's for pity
she asked you to help for pity

The Watchman starts to move some stuff.

or some other reason

Chorus
you are full of envy

Watchman
is that right?

Chorus
all those years on the hill
it did something to your soul
you don't like seeing us having something good
you like us to be the downtrodden

Watchman
listen to me
I'm your friend
I'm just saying there is something odd here
that's all
so take care

The Chorus don't like this thought; it makes them uncomfortable.

Ianthe comes on.

Ianthe
have you seen Electra?

Watchman
why? what's happened?

Ianthe
she was supposed to be in her room

Chorus
haven't seen her

Ianthe
oh hell

Watchman
calm down

Ianthe
how can I calm down?
I'm supposed to be looking after her

Chorus
she'll turn up

Ianthe
and if she doesn't?

Watchman
kids always do

Ianthe
the Queen came to me
you have to keep Electra in her room she says to me
all day she must be in her room

Chorus
she can't be part of her father coming back?

Ianthe
no

Chorus
that is what she said?

Ianthe
  and she mustn't hear anything either
  keep her windows closed

Watchman
  maybe she went around to the orchard

Ianthe
  the orchard yes

Watchman
  you'll find her

Ianthe
  of course I will
  I have never lost her before

Ianthe runs off.

The Chorus are left.

Watchman
  you see?
  why would the Queen want Electra out of the way?

Chorus
  the Queen is changed

Watchman
  I know that

Chorus
  these past few, she hasn't drunk for two days

Watchman
  absolutely
  all I am saying is it's odd that's all

The Watchman walks off.

The Chorus are left. Worried.

Chorus
  now my bones hurt again.
  oh don't start.
  my knees.

SCENE TWO

The same setting.

Agamemnon walks in. Alone.

No one seems to notice him for a second.

He is able to take it all in, watch the business.

Then Clytemnestra comes in.

She is wearing the dress he sent her.

She stands quite near him.

He sees her.

He looks back at the setting.

Agamemnon
you look incredible
all this, incredible –

Clytemnestra
a fitting celebration?

Agamemnon
more than

He looks around again.

Agamemnon
and the dress

Clytemnestra
you like it?

Agamemnon
of course I do

He steps towards her, wants to touch her.

She moves slightly.

Clytemnestra
later
this is a rehearsal now

Agamemnon
there'll be time later?

Clytemnestra
of course there will

Agamemnon
because that dress –

Clytemnestra
the rehearsal

Agamemnon
yes

Clytemnestra
are you concentrating?

Agamemnon
tell me where to stand

Clytemnestra
they'll come over and tell you
I'm not sure really
maybe here

Agamemnon
is that a shrine?

Beat.

Clytemnestra
yes, Apollo
I arranged a blessing

Agamemnon
as part of this?

Clytemnestra
    if we are to come together
    then let it be blessed

Agamemnon
    you did all this since last night?

Clytemnestra
    I called for the holy person
    I asked him to sort it

Agamemnon
    you are an incredible woman
    you did all this for me?

Clytemnestra
    for us

Agamemnon
    can't I kiss you?

Clytemnestra
    not yet.

Agamemnon
    are you sure?

Clytemnestra
    certain

He looks around.

Agamemnon
    it looks amazing, the whole place

Clytemnestra
    this has to be a spectacle
    you are the most heroic man Greece has ever known

Agamemnon
    is that what you think too?

Clytemnestra
yes of course

Her back suddenly hurts.

She nearly falls.

Clytemnestra
oww. No I am okay

Agamemnon
you're hurt –

Clytemnestra
it passes
it's just my back

She stands up again.

let me run through what will happen
you will arrive by the west gate
there will be a small crowd, I arranged for some –

Agamemnon
there are already people lining the main street

Clytemnestra
they will have to watch it from afar, I have some
    friends who are going to be here with us but
you'll walk this way towards me I'll be waiting
I'll say something like
a messenger came
three times we were told you were dead blah blah
false rumours of your death
I was in pieces blah blah
more blah blah
you get the idea

Agamemnon
have you written this out?

Clytemnestra
I have a good idea of what I am going to say
how I sat up waiting for news of you more blah
I drank a little of course etc etc
drank myself stupid

Agamemnon
are you going to use those exact words?

Clytemnestra
they will tell you that I partyed
that I lost my way, a tear or two from me

Agamemnon
I don't think you need say too much

Clytemnestra
I think we should be honest

She falls again.

He gets up, helps her.

Agamemnon
I see that you have suffered in my absence
perhaps more than I realised –

Clytemnestra
but then comes the good news people of Argos
our King
our most loved hero more blah
unnecessary of course but we have to say these things
the crowd will go crazy with applause

The Queen is now coping with a spine that is buckling.

and then the priestess says she wants us both to kneel
    in front of Apollo's shrine

Agamemnon
could someone bring something for the Queen?

Clytemnestra
you have to listen to the bit about the shrine

Agamemnon
are you sure you're alright?

Clytemnestra
she said she thought you would want to do some sort
of ritual cleansing
your father took his boots off when he came back

Agamemnon
yes he did

Clytemnestra
he asked the gods to bless the ground and the earth
the palace

Agamemnon
the sky above our heads

Clytemnestra
exactly

Agamemnon
yes of course
ritual cleansing, in front of the crowd
I like it

Clytemnestra
then hang on, yes now

She looks over to the Chorus.

oi. I've got some help for this part
wake up, friends

*The Chorus carry the purple cloths, which they put down
on the ground.*

Agamemnon
what's this?

106

Clytemnestra
I've asked them to cover the ground
so that when you walk into our house

Agamemnon
this cloth is for gods

Clytemnestra
and so you are
I hope you'll honour us by walking over them?

Agamemnon
wait –
the cleansing yes but
I am no god, did you say god?

Clytemnestra
I said we want to honour you like a god
I thought this was all

Agamemnon
my Queen, your thinking is muddled, I was away,
  too long
by which I mean you honour me too much
I can't do that

Clytemnestra
just a second
can't we talk about this?

Agamemnon
don't ask me to tread where a god should tread

Clytemnestra
they only meant to honour you
you asked for some visible sign from me

Agamemnon
seeing you here is all that I need
if I were to be greeted as a god, then the gods
  themselves would be angry
reserve these cloths for them

Clytemnestra
and disappoint the people?

Beat.

Agamemnon
what?

Clytemnestra
our people have been in war for ten years
most of them have lost brothers, sons, husbands.
you are a hero
they never get to see a god.
that is the thing.
this is the highest honour that we can give
so take it

Agamemnon has to think.

I would wrap the palace a hundred times in these
    cloths to honour you
you say everything you did you did because the gods
    asked you
fine then
be the gods' feet as you were their arm
walk for them into our house

Agamemnon
and if they should be angry?

Clytemnestra
why should they be angry?
you are their chosen one
you told me that

Agamemnon
it means this much to you?

Clytemnestra
it means this much to me.

Agamemnon
alright but I'll need help to take off my boots
even I wouldn't walk on cloths meant for gods in my
    bloody and battle-worn boots

*Clytemnestra indicates to one of the Chorus to help him
out of his boots.*

thank you
I'm not sure that my feet are any better
unwashed –

Clytemnestra
just walk

Agamemnon
alright
I'll walk
you always were bossy, I had forgotten that
let's hope I offend no one with this

He walks towards the house.

there

Clytemnestra
nice beneath the feet?

Agamemnon
nice
beautiful

*Clytemnestra's back goes again. She falls down on to
hands and knees.*

She has to crawl up.

She manages to stand, she uses her stick.

is that it?

Clytemnestra
that is it

He comes off the cloths.

Agamemnon
and then?

Clytemnestra
and then you go through the doors, I follow behind
and the crowd are beside themselves with joy and
    elation

She almost appears to retch, composes herself.

Agamemnon
have I got time for a spruce-up?

Clytemnestra
of course

Agamemnon
and this shirt. Has someone got my ceremonial suit
    ready?

Clytemnestra
it's all done

Agamemnon
as you say the country needs a display
a hero –
I can walk on the cloths of course I can

He comes back and kisses her.

clever lady@
the crowd will love it
but first a bath, a shave
even I can't be a hero with all this stubble

He goes.

Agamemnon has nearly got to the door.

oh I nearly forgot –
I have a gift here
the army gave me a gift

Clytemnestra
where?

Agamemnon
good woman step forward

He indicates towards the gate but no one steps forward.

well she is a little shy but there is a woman

Clytemnestra
you mentioned her

Agamemnon
she has been good to me all these years and I promised
   her she would be well received
she sometimes helps me when I shave

Clytemnestra
she helps you with that?

Agamemnon
well not this morning she didn't, she was a little unwell
   but
we can take her into our house can't we?

Clytemnestra
you would like that?

Agamemnon
she is nothing to me, but I can't leave her by the
   roadside
she was a gift
a sort of honour

Clytemnestra
I see

Agamemnon
a prized jewel, she was nobility in Troy

Clytemnestra
aha

Agamemnon
what would the army say if I just –

Clytemnestra
of course you must have her then

Agamemnon
you are the most wonderful woman
the most I could ask for
thank you

Agamemnon starts to go in through the door.

Happy.

and you'll like her when you get to know her

Clytemnestra speaks to the Chorus.

Clytemnestra
thank you
you did me proud, exactly as I asked
but go now, get out of here

Chorus
but you said we could stay –

Clytemnestra
not any more, I've changed my mind

Chorus
you gave us a permit –

Clytemnestra
I'll take it away

Chorus
this is our hour
our moment in the sun

Clytemnestra
it's all over
I'm warning you, get out of here

Chorus
we won't leave you

Clytemnestra
on your head be it

She sees Cassandra hovering.

come in for fuck's sake, your master has asked that
we treat you kindly here
this is no time for pride
you are lucky that we are so forgiving
you can't help that you're Trojan, we understand that

Cassandra won't move.

Chorus
she's talking to you
best to reply

Clytemnestra
maybe she can't understand me?
after all I don't speak her language

Chorus
go in with her, woman, it's the best that you can
be offered

Cassandra makes a sort of scream.

well how about that?
gratitude

She screams again.

Clytemnestra
you think I have time to stand here trying to persuade
you into my house when my husband is just home?

Chorus
I think she needs an interpreter
someone must speak her language

Cassandra screams again.

Clytemnestra
completely loopy. You see?
trust my husband to bring us a madwoman
to the asylum with you then

Cassandra
Apollo
Apollo?

Chorus
so she speaks

Clytemnestra
how can she speak, she has no tongue?

Chorus
how do you know she has no tongue?

Cassandra
Apollo gave me a new one

Clytemnestra
sorceress HOW CAN YOU TALK?

Cassandra
by Apollo's grace

Clytemnestra
I don't believe in Apollo, you witch –

Cassandra
it's you that deals in witchcraft

Clytemnestra
what, you speak again?

Cassandra
don't hurt me

Clytemnestra goes down and pulls Cassandra by the hair.

Clytemnestra
you call me a witch? twice

Cassandra
it was you that used that name
my protector Apollo will see that you putrefy

Clytemnestra
you think he cares to save you?

Cassandra
the full force of his vengeance will fall on you

Clytemnestra
he is playing with you
he gives you a gift, but takes it away
if he gives you a tongue it's only that you might lose
    it again
if there are gods let me tell you, gods we are better
    without them

Cassandra
blasphemy now heaped on your sins

Clytemnestra
no sins yet, I am clean
walk into my palace

Cassandra
walk into your palace?
freely?

Clytemnestra
why would I kill you, I have no quarrel with you
you are inconsequential
so he screwed you, so what?

Cassandra
it's my fate to be killed by you
the gods have ordained it

Clytemnestra
I don't believe in gods, fate –
what is that?

you will not die by my hand. I promise it, here in front
   of witnesses.
old men, watch this.
I am the master of my own actions, and I say she will
   not die.
walk into my house

Cassandra
   or what?

Clytemnestra
   stay in the street then
   as you wish
   you think you affect me, either way –

*The Watchman comes back, communicating with
offstage organisers.*

Watchman
   madam, we're ready to go.
   moments only.

Clytemnestra
   okay. I'll tell the King to hurry his bath

She walks into the palace.

Chorus
   foolish child to offend the Queen
   this talk of murder
   what on earth did you mean?
   you shouldn't bandy around such terms lightly
   you are a slave here
   the war with Troy is over

Cassandra
   Apollo get me out of here

Chorus
   she's crackers

Watchman
can we move her?

Cassandra
master, do you play with me?

Chorus
the Queen was right
totally nuts
deranged

The Watchman talks to the organisers.

Watchman
don't let the crowds in just yet

Cassandra
this is the house that hates the gods

Chorus
there can't be more of this raving

Cassandra
I recognise it from my nightmares
where innocent children are chopped up and fed to
    their fathers
butchery and bludgery
worshipped
the very walls are stained with blood

Watchman
we have got a bit of a problem

Chorus
she is like a wolf
she can smell everything that has gone before
how can she do that?
who has told her?

Cassandra
this house is cursed

Watchman
  oh hell

Cassandra
  it always has been, it always will be
  but today, we will see new depths
  new tidemarks of villainy.

Chorus
  someone stop her

Watchman
  help me carry her off

Cassandra
  cursed Queen, vixen of hell. How can you do that?
  to the man that has longed for you

Watchman
  I'll take you round

Cassandra
  even now as I speak she is taking his clothes, and
      stepping forward, undoing her blouse, the bath
      running
  come into the water with me she miaows like the cat
      that she is
  the bath is warm, and the embrace will be sweet she
      tells him

Chorus
  we don't understand

Cassandra
  he puts a toe under the tap to test it
  then a foot
  the water is good he nods to his wife,
  his penis already swelling the thought of a bath together
  her body, familiar but changed
  how he longs to feel her

oh to do it in the bath
evil woman
the man quite naked with no means of defence

Chorus
do what?

Cassandra
but what now, some cord
she brings some cord
he doesn't see it,
he is still looking at the water, his head already
   imagining his wife, legs astride him or from behind
she puts the cord around his wrists
what's this, a game?
he asks
she ties the string further around him
and drawing a knife
a game? he asks again
his penis larger still
he likes a game
and then the knife
the Queen gets out a knife that is meant for the kitchen
a knife that is meant for butchering a pig

Her speech is broken by screaming.

Agamemnon, naked and covered in a tangle of cord runs out of the palace.

He is limping and is caught.

Clytemnestra, half dressed, runs after him.

He is already bleeding from a gash in his side.

He trips and falls, landing like a large felled animal.

Clytemnestra
tomorrow!
tomorrow!
did you really think?

Agamemnon
  but you –

Clytemnestra
  what?
  a few soft words?
  you come back you say I can take my time, you tell
    me you have suffered. The bollocks, the self-
    righteous fucking bollocks. You have suffered,
    you have fucking suffered fucking your slave.
  she was our daughter

Agamemnon
  Clytemnestra –

Clytemnestra
  you think there's anyone around that will help you?
  a bunch of deranged misfits, a raving girl. I sent
    everyone else home.
  yes call out if you want
  flail for help as she did
  cast about, desperate
  but don't doubt that I will do this.

Agamemnon
  help please
  the Queen is not herself

Clytemnestra
  I am absolutely myself
  I was never better

She comes over with the knife.

  I gave you a test.
  what was stronger, your notion of the gods, or your
    own vanity?
  it is forbidden to walk on the gods' own cloths
  the gods have forbidden it, and if you do everything
    for them as you say

**including killing your own daughter
then why not show that same piety here?**

Agamemnon
please

Clytemnestra
it either matters or it doesn't!

Agamemnon
please stop this

Clytemnestra
you walked on the cloths, you sacrilegious pile of shit.
your beliefs are paper thin
and yet when it came to killing your own babe –

Chorus
what can we do?
we must stop this

Clytemnestra
and for what a war, another piece of vanity?
you didn't need to go to war at all
it's all about the great hero that is you

Cassandra comes to help him.

Cassandra
don't

Clytemnestra
get out of the way, someone hold her
tell me where to strike the fatal blow
you must die as she did

Agamemnon
don't die for me Cassandra, move back

Cassandra
I can't –

*Clytemnestra flails around with the knife. The Chorus
move in.*

121

She scares them off.

Chorus
get back, she'll kill you

The Chorus have grabbed Cassandra.

you tricked us too.
those cloths were part of your plan

Clytemnestra
he had a chance, I gave him a chance
if he had shown himself to be properly pious
instead he cursed himself again

Agamemnon
you've gone mad

Clytemnestra
I am full of the blood of every person sacrificed for
    the glory of another
tell me where you put the fatal blow?

Agamemnon
please my love, my –

Clytemnestra
alright, the back then the belly
must I choose where?

Agamemnon
come to your senses

Clytemnestra
where will it hurt you most?
where will you feel the most agony as you die?

Agamemnon
stop

She slices at him.

Clytemnestra
here and here

She has cut him, but not fatally.

He uses all his force and manages to overcome her.

He has her by the throat for a second.

Then she throws him off. She is stronger that he thought.

They fight savagely, both desperate. Clothes get ripped, hair pulled, teeth, nails. This is a fight to the end.

Finally, she gets the better of him.

She has him in a neck-hold.

She takes him by the head.

She has the knife at his throat.

> here I think
> here will be how it ends

Electra runs in.

Electra
Mummy?

Clytemnestra pauses.

Agamemnon
you can hear her still in your rage?

Electra
Mummy?

Clytemnestra
of course I can hear her
fucking hell, where is my servant?

Ianthe is running after her, trying to catch her.

> I told you to keep her inside

Ianthe
I tried, I lost her

Clytemnestra
get her, take her back in –

Electra
    where is Daddy, you said I could see Daddy?

Clytemnestra
    take her inside –

Agamemnon
    Electra
    is this Electra?

Electra
    I am Electra, yes.

Agamemnon
    my baby girl

Clytemnestra
    and so the moment could be sweet after all. You think?
        You think this could be a moment of open arms and
        loving embrace you think you get to have that?
    see your father Electra
    look on him for this will be your last time
    how like her sister she looks don't you think?

Agamemnon
    vixen vermin
    have you crawled from hell?

Clytemnestra
    yes and more
    beyond hell that is where I have been
    now close your eyes my darling
    sweet Electra
    turn your head
    this man is not a man you can call a father
    this man is a child killer
    shut your eyes I said
    this I don't want you to see
    someone stand with Electra
    someone make sure her eyes are shut

She talks to Ianthe.

you, shut her eyes

Ianthe
I won't

Clytemnestra
you always do what I say

Ianthe
not with this

Clytemnestra calls over to the Chorus.

Clytemnestra
you then, friends, one of you cover her eyes

Chorus
we can't
you made us impotent again
you said we were nothing

Clytemnestra
PLEASE SOMEONE
shut your eyes Electra, you should not see this
someone somebody stand behind her

Ianthe has joined the Chorus – they won't help.

The ghost of Iphigenia comes out from the shadows.

She stands behind her sister Electra.

She puts her hands over her eyes.

alright, those that want no part in this look away –
those that want to sleep well tonight turn your head
none of you are my friends

Agamemnon
no

Clytemnestra slits Agamemnon's throat.

125

There is a sort of breathy moan from the Chorus, or is it the earth itself that screams out?

Clytemnestra holds up Agamemnon's head.

Clytemnestra
behold your hero
behold your vanquishing King.
behold King Agamemnon, the butcher of children

The Chorus are in disarray.

Chorus
cursed woman
you won't get away with it

Clytemnestra
I think I just did –

Chorus
the crowd are not far

Clytemnestra
what you think they will come and fight me? You
    have been old too long

Chorus
we must call for help
raise an army

Clytemnestra laughs.

Clytemnestra
an army, led by you?

Chorus
this is the first step towards tyranny

Clytemnestra
it was justice that was done here, and you helped me

Chorus
don't bring us into this
what can we do?

Clytemnestra
rejoice, that is what you can do!
celebrate with me
I did it
I did what my girl demanded
I may have failed as a mother in many ways
I may have not noticed or by looking the other way
I let her be killed in the first place, not realising the
    threat
I failed her then.
but not today.
today I did this.
this was my mother's work and it is done.
so let's get drunk
for every woman that harbours a doubt
for every woman who worries in silence
drink with me

Chorus
she's deranged
brazen

Clytemnestra turns to Cassandra.

Clytemnestra
and look I have the blood of one on my hands not two.
I changed my fate
I have free will

*Cassandra shows her she has been gashed and is bleeding
from the belly.*

but there is no fight with you –
who did this to you?

Cassandra
you did, madam, as you flailed with the knife

Clytemnestra
no

127

Cassandra falls back, bleeding.

NO

Clytemnestra falls to her, picks her up.

you will not die. Do not die to spite me
keep breathing.
damn you
you are not supposed to die here –

Cassandra slumps.

no no no
someone help me, help her

Ianthe is now part of the Chorus.

Chorus
you have no friends here

Clytemnestra
she is an innocent, another innocent

She cradles Cassandra.

you cannot be dead

Chorus
it was written by the gods
and you said there was no such thing

Clytemnestra
don't frighten me

A man, Aegisthus, comes in, through the gate.

Aegisthus
I have a permit for fuck's sake

This is

He sees the scene.

Aegisthus
so you did it –

Clytemnestra doesn't answer him.

Clytemnestra
you didn't think I would

Aegisthus
and it's properly done?

Clytemnestra
the King is dead, if that is proper

Aegisthus
well done

Clytemnestra
not well done at all.
look at this, another victim

Aegisthus
a slave

Clytemnestra
I shouldn't have killed her, I was not supposed to
kill her

Aegisthus comes over to Cassandra, looks at her.

Aegisthus
it doesn't matter

Clytemnestra
I wanted it to be different

Aegisthus
you should have let me do it

Clytemnestra
perhaps I was wrong, perhaps the gods after all

Aegisthus
many times I would have done it

Clytemnestra
she wasn't supposed to die here

Aegisthus
for revenge

Clytemnestra
whose?

Aegisthus
my darling, you aren't thinking straight
yours of course
but mine too when his father boiled and served up
my brothers

Clytemnestra
what if I had hesitated?

Aegisthus
I would have come in behind you

Clytemnestra
oh hell the rain
did you feel it? I felt rain

Chorus
you've forgotten about us
we may be old

Aegisthus laughs.

Aegisthus
this is the day of justice
for the Queen and for myself
can't you see?

Chorus
this isn't justice
we may not be able to fight, but we can tell a story,
and tell everyone of what we have seen

Aegisthus
you seem to miss the point

Chorus
there are six of us

Ianthe
seven

Aegisthus looks at them. Registers the dissent, then goes over to them, takes Ianthe in a headlock.

Clytemnestra
Aegisthus – look at the sky

Aegisthus
they say they are serious
I should do them the honour of taking them at their
word

Clytemnestra
they don't matter –

Aegisthus
a story will be told about how he met his end.
and we will all tell it

He is hurting Ianthe, quite badly.

Chorus
stop

Aegisthus
she needs to say that she'll tell it

Ianthe is being hurt. She yelps.

Chorus
you're hurting her

Aegisthus
she is one of your number now, protect her

He hurts her even more. Ianthe screams in agony.

Chorus
alright we'll say it

Aegisthus
the King fell in the bathroom. He hit his head.

Chorus
the King fell in the bathroom he hit his head

Aegisthus turns to Ianthe.

Aegisthus
and you?

Ianthe
he fell

Aegisthus
I didn't hear you

Ianthe
he fell

Aegisthus
you saw him?

Chorus/Ianthe
we all did

Aegisthus looks at them all.

Aegisthus
your revolt seemed to fall at the first test

He laughs, then wonders if he can trust them.

maybe we should just finish this?

Clytemnestra
no, let them go –
look, the skies are turning black

Aegisthus
it would only take one of them to break their word

Clytemnestra
there has been enough here today.
quick let's get in

Aegisthus
they are weeds these people

Chorus
you may have silenced us but the gods won't like it

Aegisthus
the gods?

Clytemnestra
who speaks of the gods?

Aegisthus
you and I hold the power in this house.
together or not

Chorus
blasphemy

Aegisthus
get out of here
out of my sight

The Chorus start to move off.

*Aegisthus scares them away, with a growl like a dog.
They run.*

He comes back to Clytemnestra.

Clytemnestra
we need to go inside. A storm is starting up –

Aegisthus
I won't be cowed by men like them.
anyway, we have timing on our side. Everyone is sick
of fighting. And the women are too tired.
they are fucking each other senseless tonight, who
cares what happened here?
all anyone wants is a strong city, and we will give
them that

Clytemnestra
I want to go in

Aegisthus
alright, we can start rebuilding Argos tomorrow

Clytemnestra
tomorrow?

Aegisthus
yes, tomorrow
when all the good things will begin

Clytemnestra
together?

Aegisthus
whatever you want, step in step
or side by side

He offers his hand, she takes it.

The rain starts in earnest.

Clytemnestra
oh hell

Aegisthus
hang on to me, be steady

Clytemnestra
don't you see? This is a new curse

Aegisthus
it is just some weather, a little shower

Clytemnestra
why now though, why on us?

Aegisthus
come lady

Aegisthus tries to get her to walk into the palace.

Clytemnestra remembers her daughter. She breaks free.

Clytemnestra
Electra.
Electra come with us

Electra doesn't answer.

Electra, baby –
Please? Come inside with us.

Aegisthus
she will in her own time

Clytemnestra
but she's part of it, part of our future

Aegisthus
she'll come, won't you?

Clytemnestra
darling?

Electra doesn't answer.

Aegisthus
she is too young to have understood
come on, let's get you inside first

Clytemnestra shouts as she goes.

Clytemnestra
don't stay in the rain –

They walk in without her.

Electra is left alone on stage apart from the two dead bodies.

The rain falls heavily.

Electra comes down to her father.

She picks up her father's body, and cradles it.

Iphigenia comes and cradles her.

She rocks her. She smooths her hair.

She speaks into her sister's ear. It almost sounds like a lullaby.

Iphigenia
cleanse the spirit with Guelder Rose.
Hibiscus, Hawthorn to bring you luck
Thyme and Marigold to help you dream
Sweet Linden to forget

The rain continues.

PART TWO

THE BOUGH BREAKS

Characters

The Butcher
Celia
Clytemnestra
Electra
Aegisthus
A Doctor
Orestes

SCENE ONE

The Palace Butcher comes on to the stage.

He starts making a cup of tea.

Butcher
    the doctor said perhaps she was too hot –
    so we opened all the windows in the room
    the doctor said perhaps she was too cold –
    so we lit a fire
    the doctor said try a little soup
    so we made soup
    try a little cold compress on the skin, he said
    try a hot compress on the skin
    try needles beneath the fingernails
    feathers on the feet
    trumpets in the ear
    nothing
    not one twitch
    not a single moment where she sat up and looked at us
    the doctor at least is honest, I have never seen this
       before, he said, it's a mystery
    I read all the books, then I read them again

Beat.

    so the King starts – this has to be sorted now
    he has a sign put up in the town
    has to be careful,
    no one really likes them out there
    there was celebrating I heard, the Queen won't wake
    thank fuck
    let's light a fire, dance around it

let's hope she dies that way
but the King puts on his notice
a huge reward
anyone that can rouse her from her sleep
they came then, they lined up outside the palace
little old women
little old men
the young, the weird
the slap bang ordinary
try this, it woke my child
pray to this god, it cured the lame
a different potion, a different prayer for every hour
none of it worked, of course
the King, by now in a temper
get out you stupid cretins
get out get out, can no one wake my wife?

Beat.

I should have introduced myself
I am the butcher here
I was the butcher, been the butcher since the age of ten
most of the staff ran that night
most of them couldn't get out of here fast enough
blood on the flagstones, get gone
but me
well, where else had I to go?
I was the butcher before
what was I going to be after?
I am the cook, the cleaner now
anything that needs doing
I make her a cup of tea every hour
on the hour so that when she wakes
well, she'll be thirsty after a sleep like that

A serving woman, Celia, comes in.

She looks at the Butcher, he looks at her.

Celia
don't know why you bother

Butcher
don't start

Celia
seventeen days, the situation is clear

Butcher
she'll wake up

Celia
tff
you said that yesterday and the day before
if she was going to wake she would have done by now

She picks up a pile of sheets and goes out.

you should be digging a grave not making the tea

The Butcher is left with the cup and saucer.

SCENE TWO

In the Queen's bedroom.

The Butcher brings in the cup of tea.

Electra is watching her mother.

The Butcher puts down the tea.

He starts to go.

Electra
please don't just leave

The Butcher looks uncomfortable.

Butcher
where's the King?

Electra

the King is no use
you are the closest she's got to a friend

He looks at her.

I mean, I know I'm not supposed to talk to staff but
I've been here for ten hours
on my own
and
my mother is fond of you
I know you work in the kitchen

Butcher

worked there all my life

Electra

I know you cleaned the flagstones
that night

Beat.

I know everyone else ran pretty much but you got out
a bucket and cleaned the blood off the flagstones
you didn't need to

Beat.

and I know you put me to bed
I don't remember anything of that night, but my mum
told me
she pointed you out in the garden one day when you
were dragging a calf and said that man there, he put
you to bed that night
that dreadful night
he is one you can trust
he lifted you up from the flagstones once he had
finished cleaning them and he carried you up to
your room

Beat.

144

Butcher
    I only did –

Electra
    I just mean –
    that was nice
    I might have stayed out there all night if it wasn't
        for you

Beat.

    you're different to the rest
    oh they do what they are told but they
    well you get the feeling they despise us
    but you –
    for some reason you aren't like that

Beat.

    she looks exactly the same doesn't she? No better no
        worse

Butcher
    here, you have the tea

Electra
    it would be better if we were a normal family
    things like this happen in a normal family and you
        can go, okay
    this is something to do with the body
    the blood or the veins something in the sinews
    this belongs in the physical world
    but in our family –

Butcher
    the doctor will find a cure

Electra
    the King is thinking of sacking the doctor
    he has no patience
    he will be imprisoned and beaten before long

Butcher
   he'll get another doctor, a better doctor

Electra
   we both know what this is.
   don't look at me like that I'm not an idiot
   this is a haunting.

Beat.

   don't tell me it isn't
   you of all people should know that
   it started on the anniversary, a thousand days
   I can't be the only one that noticed that

Butcher
   I think you should talk to the King

Electra
   the King is stupid, can only see what the King sees
   I say to him this is a haunting, he'll laugh in my face
   you know where the grave is

Butcher
   Electra

Electra
   I love my mother, I won't let her die
   and the stupid doctor can't offer her anything
   she needs us to end this

Butcher
   how?

Electra
   by going to the grave
   by calling the ghost

Beat.

Butcher
   you know talk of ghosts is outlawed

Electra
I know

Butcher
the gods don't like it
once a spirit has crossed the river that is that. Men
do not come back to earth to do ill

Electra
and yet you hear of it

Butcher
those are stories, older stories.
the two are incompatible
your father is in the underworld
he cannot harm anyone

Electra
and yet he does

Beat.

Butcher
your mother in particular is very clear about the gods
she is a devout observer now. Look at the shrines to
Athena she has here in her room

Electra
she wasn't always, she used to laugh at the gods
she told me about a ghost who sat on her shoulder once

Beat.

Butcher
we couldn't even get to the grave
no one is allowed out of the palace grounds
you know you step out you might get killed

Electra
another objection

Butcher
that the King has given these orders

147

Electra
the King again

Butcher
there are enemies all around
people plotting –

Electra
we can be safe, we'll cover our heads
we'll go in disguise
if she would just wake on her own okay, but –
I have to go to the grave
listen I'm not asking you to believe it, I'm just asking
you to take me to the grave

Butcher
if I get caught, I am a servant here

Electra
I am no better

Butcher
the King won't punish you

Electra
you think?
you don't know how cruel the King can be
it's an unmarked grave, I won't find it without you

The Butcher hesitates.

forget it then.
please excuse me, I thought you were someone
you're not.
I have finished my tea

She hands him back her cup.

Butcher
I didn't say that

Electra
so what did you say?

Aegisthus comes in.

Aegisthus
time for you to go

Electra
aren't you going to ask how she is?

Aegisthus takes his shoes off and gets on to the bed.

Aegisthus
a little worse by the looks of things

Electra
she is exactly the same

He looks at Clytemnestra.

Aegisthus
a little worse
did you move my stuff off the bed?

Electra
no

Aegisthus
my nightshirt, I sleep here
why is my stuff on the floor?

Electra
it fell

Aegisthus
what, she rolled over and it fell?

Electra
I moved it a little, I thought she looked uncomfortable

Aegisthus
don't touch her
I told you before, she isn't yours

Aegisthus cuddles into her.

she seems worse
what did you do to her?

Electra
nothing, I spoke to her that's all

Aegisthus
you spoke to her?

Electra
yes. I spoke to her all day

Aegisthus
I don't think you should be alone with her any more

Electra
what?

Aegisthus
I think only the doctors and I should attend to her
from now on

Electra
she is my mother

Aegisthus
and she is my wife
I am in charge in this house

Electra
she is in charge

Aegisthus
she is asleep
I think it's better if you stay away
you're making her worse by your presence

Electra
she is exactly the same as this morning

Aegisthus
are you arguing with me?

Electra
no

Aegisthus
I'll decide what is best for her
thank you
stay away, Electra, or I will keep you out.

Electra
you can't do that

Aegisthus
I am king here
you were tolerated while your mother was here, but
    now she's not.

Electra
she is here

Aegisthus
she is asleep.

Beat.

and while she sleeps

Electra
I hate you.

Aegisthus
I think I'll live
now get out of here before I call someone to remove
    you.

Electra
no

Aegisthus
no?

Electra
she needs me here

Aegisthus
oh so you want me to use some force?

He slaps Electra. Electra's face stings.

She picks up the teacup to throw. The Butcher intervenes to stop her.

Butcher
come, Electra, come with me

Electra
I hate him

Butcher
don't fight
we've got things to do.
come on.

Aegisthus
a wise servant with some sense
shut the door behind you

Butcher
come on

The Butcher takes Electra's hand.

SCENE THREE

The Butcher and Electra are outside.

They have come to a stop some distance from the palace in a patch of rough ground.

Butcher
families can be difficult places
a new father on the scene –

Electra
he isn't my father, and he isn't that new

Butcher
your mother ill
just let me get my bearings

He looks about.

Electra
I wish someone would kill him
you say we have enemies
I would open the door

Butcher
they hate your mother worse, sorry to say

Electra
I know

Butcher
he'll settle down
when your mother is better. You know the truth?
he is as worried as you, he doesn't know how to
    handle it

Electra
and me? Why should I be the one who knows how
    to handle it?

Butcher
keep your voice down
if anyone heard us talking like this –

Electra
there's no one around

Butcher
oh they'll be out there
watching
and when they ask

Electra
you're paranoid

Butcher
you are my granddaughter
when anyone asks
we've come out for a walk

Electra doesn't answer.

    we aren't looking for anything in particular
    we like nature
    butterflies in fact
    we like walking through the fields

Electra
    this is crazy –

Butcher
    looking for butterflies
    that's why we are here
    we are out enjoying a day in the fields

Electra
    what would they do? These people

Butcher
    me? They would string me up from the nearest tree
    you?
    I don't like to think what they would do to you.

Electra
    why have we stopped here?

Butcher
    I'm trying to remember
    it is one of these

Electra
    here?

Butcher
    of these three
    two
    it could be this one or that one

Electra
    you don't remember?

Butcher
    it was dark
    we didn't have long, we had to move him, we knew
        there'd be trouble

The Butcher looks around.

    we marked it with a few stones but I –

He looks at the ground.

Electra
    it isn't going to work if we aren't even sure

Butcher
    I can't guarantee

Electra
    so what, am I supposed to pour wine into all the
        mounds on this stretch?

Butcher
    you asked me to take you to the grave

Electra
    yes to the grave
    not to the general vicinity

Butcher
    I wish you would keep your voice down

Electra
    there is no one
    I can't see a single person, look

Butcher
    they'll be hiding, they won't be in full view
    they'll be watching us though

Electra looks around.

Electra
    well I don't care

Butcher
      stop it, this isn't a joke
      why are you so fearless?

Electra
      is that a crime?

Butcher
      sit down.
      please, now we are here, let's do it quickly

Electra sits down and undoes her bag.

Electra
      I haven't exactly thought through what I am going
            to say so you are going to have to give me a little
            leeway

Butcher
      of course

Electra
      I wasn't talking to you

She takes out some wine and some oil.

      thing is –

She pauses for a second to consider what to say.

      okay, we hardly know each other
      and the things I know aren't good
      but, you are my dad and
      this has to stop
      whatever it is you are doing to Mum, could you stop?

She is suddenly self-conscious.

      maybe I should sing, do you think I should sing?

Butcher
      bit noisy –

Electra
how can I talk to him? I don't know him

Butcher
say the first thing that comes into your head –

Electra
it would be easiest of all if I could say she was sorry
she didn't mean it
she lost her head and went crazy

Butcher
so say she is sorry

Electra
but, she isn't
is she?
she thinks the gods have damned her but
she has told everyone she would do it again
and he believes –

Butcher
he's dead

Electra
I know

Beat.

She looks at the grave.

what was he like?

Butcher
complicated

Electra
no difference there then
maybe this was dumb
he doesn't know me, I don't know him
maybe there isn't much I can say actually

Butcher
    you can soothe

Electra
    with what?

Butcher
    with being here
    we came this far

Beat.

The Butcher sits down beside her.

    you're doing well

Beat.

Electra
    Dad
    I . . .
    Dad I guess
    I don't understand you and I don't understand her
    but could you be calmer?
    let go a bit
    do something about your anger
    there must be better things to do over there
    fun things
    new things
    can't you go and do some of those?
    you were loved, I think
    you are loved even
    there is nothing to be gained by taking her too
    I need her here
    I need her to be well
    here
    because if I don't have her –
    so leave her now, please
    and let her wake up
    that's what I came to say. Dad

158

really, that is all
I lost my sister, I lost you
I don't want to lose my mum as well.

Beat.

do you think that's okay?

Butcher
I think that's probably okay

Electra
do I have to pour the rest of the wine in?

Butcher
you might as well

Electra
maybe we should have brought more
I don't like the way it makes the ground sort of bubble

Butcher
what was that?

Electra
what?

The Butcher stands up.

Butcher
I heard a noise

Electra
just me
clinking the bottle

Butcher
if someone is coming

Electra
where? There's nothing

Butcher
over there

Electra
  there's no one

Butcher
  someone is watching us and making a noise

Electra
  this is my father's grave I am not afraid
  it's the bell you can hear

Butcher
  what bell?

Electra
  the bell from the palace

The Butcher looks around.

Butcher
  what?

They listen.

Electra
  something has happened.

SCENE FOUR

Clytemnestra is standing up.

The serving woman, Celia, is changing her from her nightdress.

Aegisthus and a Doctor are in attendance. The Doctor is a nervous man who is feeling the pressure.

Clytemnestra
  I feel –

The Doctor and Aegisthus wait expectantly for her to finish her sentence.

She can't.

She tries again.

I feel –

Again she comes to a stop.

The Doctor and Aegisthus forward.

Again she comes to a stop.

Doctor
maybe don't try and speak just yet

Aegisthus
what is it, what does she feel?

Doctor
I don't know, would you give me a second –

Aegisthus
is there something wrong?

Doctor
I think we have to wait and give her time

Clytemnestra
I feel –

Beat.

Doctor
perhaps she is thirsty, could she have some water?

Aegisthus
water!

Doctor
and some softened fruit

Aegisthus
you think that will help?

Doctor
of course it will

A glass of water is brought.

They look at her again.

She drinks the water.

Clytemnestra
I feel absolutely –

Beat.

Doctor
dizzy perhaps?

Clytemnestra
dizzy no

Doctor
let me take your pulse

Aegisthus
is all okay?

Doctor
I'm trying to check

Aegisthus
well check quicker

The Doctor feels for her pulse.

Beat.

Then he feels it again.

well?

Doctor
it's remarkable

Clytemnestra
could I have a bath?

Aegisthus
can he see your teeth?
look at her teeth, look in her mouth

Doctor
  I am I am

Aegisthus
  look at her all over

Clytemnestra
  is this necessary?

Aegisthus
  he must check all possibilities
  you nearly bloody died

She shows her teeth.

Doctor
  entirely normal

Aegisthus
  show him your hands

Clytemnestra
  I feel like an animal

Doctor
  she has a slight sweat on her palms

Aegisthus
  is that a catastrophe?

Doctor
  I don't know how to read it

Clytemnestra
  is that all?

Doctor
  there doesn't appear to be much wrong with her,
    it appears . . .

Clytemnestra
  I do have a slight headache

Aegisthus
a slight headache
did you hear that?

Doctor
I'll note it down

Clytemnestra
it's minor

Aegisthus
nothing is minor

The Doctor looks at her.

Doctor
something miraculous has happened here. I don't
mind telling you now I was worried, but look at
the woman

Clytemnestra
can I get dressed now, can I walk about?

Doctor
sir, I believe your wife is fine

Aegisthus takes this in.

as inexplicable as it is, she has woken up
entirely herself

Aegisthus
really?
she's fine?

Doctor
I believe she is

He smiles and they sort of laugh together.

Clytemnestra
well how long did I sleep for?

Doctor
too long

Aegisthus kisses her, then talks to the Doctor.

Aegisthus
you'll be well rewarded, whatever you want

Doctor
that is very kind –

Aegisthus
just stay close if you would

The Doctor starts to retreat.

there is a thing – just as you said whatever I want

Aegisthus
later

There is some threat now in Aegisthus' voice.

Beat.

Doctor
absolutely

The Doctor goes.

Aegisthus kisses Clytemnestra.

Aegisthus
you don't know how worried I was
you fucking terrified me, come here, you

Clytemnestra
there's a fly on my shirt

Aegisthus
my sweet sweet girl

Clytemnestra
can you get it off

Aegisthus
what?

Clytemnestra
    that fly
    you know I hate flies

He brushes it off.

Aegisthus
    well done for waking up, whatever the hell that was
    bloody hell, and I missed you,
    don't ever sleep like that again, I need you

Electra rushes in.

Electra
    what's happened?

Clytemnestra
    my baby

Electra
    what? You woke up

She runs to hug her mother.

    you just woke up by yourself?

Clytemnestra
    yes

Electra
    I thought you'd die

Aegisthus
    we all thought that

Clytemnestra
    come here, baby

Aegisthus
    don't crowd her

Clytemnestra
    she's okay

Aegisthus
you've been extremely ill
I don't think she should rush at you like that

Clytemnestra
it's fine

Aegisthus
the doctor said –

Clytemnestra
the doctor said I was entirely myself

Electra
are you really okay?

Clytemnestra
I am, I think, completely normal.
apart from a slight headache

Electra laughs.

come on, the two of you.
I'm okay. Let me hug you both

Aegisthus joins in the hug. The three of them for a second.

Electra
will you come outside with me? The sun is shining

Clytemnestra
now?

Electra
why not?

Clytemnestra looks at Aegisthus.

Clytemnestra
shall we all go outside?

Aegisthus
I think it's a bit wet to go outside
you've been extremely unwell

Electra
the rain has passed

Aegisthus
but underfoot –

Electra
she can wear some shoes

Clytemnestra
we could just go out for a minute, couldn't we?

Aegisthus
and then?
risk ill health?

Beat.

Clytemnestra
I'll come out later, Electra love

Beat.

Electra
its okay, I'll stay indoors then

Aegisthus
no reason why you shouldn't go outside –

Electra
I want to be with her

Clytemnestra
good, all three of us together

She takes both of their hands.

I love you both

Aegisthus
I have some work to do

Clytemnestra
    now?

Aegisthus
    yes now
    I'll see you later

He leaves them.

Clytemnestra watches him go. Worried.

SCENE FIVE

The Butcher is in the kitchen making a cup of tea.

Celia
    what are you doing?

Butcher
    I make this every hour

Celia
    she's woken up now

Butcher
    I know but –

Celia takes the cup out of his hand.

Celia
    it's over

Butcher
    maybe she would still like a cup of tea

Celia
    she's in the garden with her daughter
    look

The Butcher looks.

    do you ever think you care too much, that you are
        too involved?

Butcher
I've been here a long time that's all

Celia
it's more than that
it's like you think of them before you think of yourself
everyone else ran, but you –

Butcher
I had nowhere else to go

Celia
you had plenty places
I know your sister
she'd have taken you in like a shot
you couldn't go
something about you

Butcher
and?
you say that like it is a character flaw

Celia
it's an observation.
you're different to me
you get too close and you don't seem to notice.
come on, I'll make you a cup of tea

SCENE SIX

Aegisthus and Clytemnestra are at dinner.

Some formality to the dining room, but otherwise the atmosphere is drab.

Aegisthus
how are you now?

Clytemnestra
you need to stop fussing

Aegisthus
   just tell me you are still fine

Clytemnestra
   I am still fine

Aegisthus
   remarkable

Beat.

Clytemnestra
   where's Electra?
   I thought Electra might be joining us

Aegisthus
   no, did you want her?
   I just thought
   well, some time alone, just the –

Clytemnestra
   oh

Beat.

Aegisthus
   do you mind?

Clytemnestra
   not at all.
   that's lovely

Beat.

   where will she eat?

Aegisthus
   she'll eat in the kitchen
   she seems to like the staff and
   well, it's late for Electra, you always say she goes
      to bed too late so I thought tonight –

Clytemnestra
   you are so thoughtful

Beat.

Aegisthus
shall I serve?

Clytemnestra
thank you.

Aegisthus
how much would you like?

Clytemnestra
some

He serves her.

He serves himself.

He tucks in.

She doesn't.

He looks at her.

She looks at him.

They smile.

Then he starts eating again.

She doesn't.

Aegisthus
something wrong?

Clytemnestra
no

She tries again.

Aegisthus
is it too greasy?
too cold, do you want me to get them to heat it up?

Clytemnestra
no I . . .

Beat.

there's an insect of some sort in fact

Aegisthus
where?

Clytemnestra
here
on my plate

Aegisthus
I'll get that imbecile in the kitchen beaten

Clytemnestra
no
don't do that

She holds the insect up on her fork.

it's interesting that is all
another fly

Aegisthus reaches over and takes the fly off her plate.

Aegisthus
there it's gone

She looks down at her plate.

She starts to eat.

Aegisthus
you know while you were away

Clytemnestra
I wasn't away

Aegisthus
I mean asleep
it was like you were away
while you were asleep
I tried to keep things going but
I actually had no appetite

the things about governance came up, several things
I realised I

Clytemnestra
and now there is another

Aegisthus
what?

Clytemnestra
there's another fly

Aegisthus
the same one

Clytemnestra
no another, here
in my food

He stops, he looks over at her plate.

Aegisthus
I can't see it

Clytemnestra
you can't see that?

He looks.

Aegisthus
it's tiny

Clytemnestra
I had this dream

Aegisthus
can I talk to you about the governance?

Clytemnestra
sorry

Aegisthus
no go on, your dream

Clytemnestra
    I dreamt I was being chased by flies
    all over the fields
    I was outside the palace
    walking through the fields
    hot day
    but these flies
    and the more I ran the more there were of them

Aegisthus
    just a dream

Clytemnestra
    I know but –

Beat.

    then the first thing I saw when I opened my eyes
        that fly on my shirt

Aegisthus
    it's May

Clytemnestra
    three flies in a short space of time?

Aegisthus
    you should see the flies around the cattle at this time
        of year

Beat.

Aegisthus
    we all have dreams
    whatever that sleep was, well it was odd –

Clytemnestra
    there's something rotten here
    why was it my plate that they fell on and not yours
    why was it my sleeve?

Aegisthus
    I think you are reading too much into this

Clytemnestra
I am damned, I know I am damned
the gods have told me I am damned but
now –
well why are the flies attracted to me not you?

Aegisthus
you're confused, maybe you are still coming out
    of your sleep

Clytemnestra
I never felt more awake
apart from this damn headache

She stands up.

look there they are on the ceiling
they are waiting for me, ready to pounce
what brings flies but dead flesh?
that was what the dream was telling me
I'm going to be dead soon

Aegisthus
listen, we can call a seer –

Clytemnestra
I don't need a seer –

Aegisthus
there might be an alternative explanation

Clytemnestra
to what?
the gods have condemned me for my crime

She puts a hand out.

see they fly towards me now

Aegisthus
you know this talk is really turning my stomach
okay, so you were tired or had some illness but now

there is nothing wrong with you madam the doctor
    said himself

Clytemnestra
so why are they all around me?

Aegisthus
they aren't
there is nothing around you but imagination

Clytemnestra
the gods –

Aegisthus
the gods nothing, it was necessary what you did
sit back down

She doesn't.

alright, let us eat standing up

He stands up.

He holds his plate.

I try with you
I really do
you've been asleep for over two weeks, don't you think
    that might have been a little hard for me too?
don't you think I might have been a bit worried about
    you?
don't you think I might have been dumped with
    the governance and your daughter and you sleeping
    sweetly?
I'm not saying I mind it is just
now you're awake
now you are awake

Beat.

I thought this could be a little time for us

Clytemnestra
even if the gods have made me rot?

Aegisthus
you aren't rotting. That's the point
you know I wish you would just say what is actually
    going on here.
you don't want to spend time with me
you might as well be honest
this is nothing to do with the gods
even an evening, even the short distance of a meal
    is too much for you to bear

Clytemnestra
that isn't true

Aegisthus
you asked about Electra, you would prefer her to
    be here

Clytemnestra
she is my daughter

Aegisthus
even before you went to sleep things were difficult
we both know it
at the start it was bearable perhaps with some
    moments of lightness but after that, these past
    three years

Clytemnestra
yes we had problems but –

Aegisthus
it was more than that

Beat.

you won't even look at me now
this evening since you woke up

Clytemnestra
I'll look at you

Aegisthus
  when asked
  I tried to kiss you before, you turned your head

Clytemnestra
  Electra was there

Aegisthus
  Electra is always there
  I am not blind, when I touch you you shiver, when
    I come near you you back away

Clytemnestra
  you're too sensitive

Aegisthus
  tell me I am wrong then

Clytemnestra
  can we not just eat our meal?

Aegisthus
  if we could just eat yes –
  my point exactly
  if we could eat then yes

Clytemnestra
  alright you tell me what other meaning can there be
    in these flies?

Aegisthus
  for fuck's sake, enough!

Clytemnestra
  why are you so angry?

Aegisthus
  you know what I really think? All this I am troubled,
    I don't sleep, I sleep too long, I have dreams, the
    flies, the gods, I must atone
  you never believed any of that shit –

Clytemnestra
but I was wrong –

Aegisthus
bollocks – it's an act
you want me to believe you are crazed, bewildered
you see meaning where there is none
I won't fall for it

Clytemnestra
what do you mean?

Aegisthus
you want to keep me out

Clytemnestra
it is always about sex

Aegisthus
yes I desire you
I am your husband I want you
badly, I want you

Clytemnestra
and me? If I am not in the mood –

Aegisthus
you are never in the mood, that is just it

Clytemnestra
that isn't true

Aegisthus
then prove me wrong.

Clytemnestra
you will excuse me. I have tired of this conversation

Aegisthus
of course you have

Clytemnestra walks out.

I fucking love you, you know that.
I just want you to love me back

He smashes over the flowers.

SCENE SEVEN

Later. In the middle of the night.

Clytemnestra goes downstairs to the kitchen.

Clytemnestra
hello?

She looks around.

is anyone awake?

The woman Celia comes.

I'm looking for the butcher

Celia
he . . .

Clytemnestra
I realise it is late
it's the middle of the night
and I understand he might be asleep
but could you wake him

Celia stops for a second.

please

Celia goes.

Clytemnestra looks around the kitchen.

She looks at the knives.

She doesn't like the look of them.

She moves the block further away from herself.

181

The Butcher comes out, dishevelled, pulling a cardigan over his night gear.

Butcher
madam
I am sorry I am –

Clytemnestra
I can't sleep

Butcher
that isn't surprising

Clytemnestra
I know, of course I have slept too much but
in the past you have made me a little poultice

Butcher
a poultice?

Clytemnestra
I don't mind not sleeping but
something to relax perhaps
when I needed to . . .
some herbs or something
in the old days I would drink but obviously

Butcher
of course

Clytemnestra
or maybe I could just sit with you
the house is asleep

Butcher
it's the middle of the night

Clytemnestra
I know
some herbs then
a poultice, yes please

Butcher
  I'll start right now

He looks around.

He gets a knife out.

She watches him.

Clytemnestra
  I can smell this awful stench

Butcher
  in here?

Clytemnestra
  everywhere
  and it comes from me

Butcher
  no

Clytemnestra
  it's like my flesh is starting to rot, I told the King but he –
  I tried to look in the mirror
  is there a fly on my back?

Butcher
  is there a fly . . . ?

Clytemnestra
  I asked the woman upstairs they said they couldn't
    see anything but I don't think they looked properly

She pulls down up shirt.

  can you see something there?

Butcher
  you want me to look?

Clytemnestra
  yes of course, look

The Butcher looks.

Butcher
no

Clytemnestra
look again

Butcher
I am looking

Clytemnestra
I can feel them
there are things crawling across my skin, eating the
rot –
I'm worried they're laying eggs that there will be
maggots soon in my skin
and then the maggots will turn into adults and I will
have a hundred flies on my back

He puts a hand on her.

Butcher
here

Clytemnestra
ouch, yes and lower
smell it, I smell rotten
don't be afraid to tell me –
please scrape it away
if you find the fly kill it

Butcher
there's nothing there

Clytemnestra
scrape it away –

Butcher
with what?

Clytemnestra
I don't care with what
with your hand –

He takes the knife.

He scrapes the flies off her back.

harder, you don't need to worry about cutting me
harder.

Butcher
madam

Clytemnestra
you're my servant
get the flies off my back.

He scrapes them away.

I always knew I would have to die
we always know that
it's the human condition to know that one day all
    this will be gone but
I thought I would have a little more time
I thought I would be able to raise Electra

Butcher
you will

Clytemnestra
I thought I would be able to pray hard and make
    amends

Butcher
of course

Clytemnestra
I thought I would go to my grave not as damned as
    I am
I thought I would be forgiven
but my death now
well, eternity is a long time to be dragging my soul
what will they do to me if I am to die now?

Butcher
who?

Clytemnestra
    the gods
    that's who has sent the smell
    they're telling me my time is up

Butcher
    madam I think this is just interpretation

Clytemnestra
    I know as clearly as I know anything.
    will you look after Electra?

He puts the knife back down.

Butcher
    of course I will.

Clytemnestra
    you dropped something

Butcher
    where?

Clytemnestra
    there, you dropped it
    pick it up
    if the gods are saying my time is coming
    you can't be dropping things

Butcher
    I didn't drop anything

Clytemnestra
    sorry, I thought you did
    it's me then
    its me that is dropping things

She stoops down. She sees that there is nothing there.

She stands back up.

    I don't want to die yet

SCENE EIGHT

Next morning.

Electra goes back to the grave. She is alone this time.

Electra
    that wasn't supposed to happen.
    if that was some sort of joke?
    I didn't ask you to wake her just to make her worse –
    what the hell are you doing?
    I brought more wine, I don't know if that was what
        you wanted or
    the men in the garden said you preferred spirits
    so
    here, get drunk
    spend eternity in a stupor
    please don't do this
    I'm calling on you, ghost
    this is not fair, if this is a joke?

A Man calls over from a little way away.

Man
    you shouldn't be here

Electra
    I . . .

Man
    no one should be here
    do you know how dangerous it is?

Electra
    I was just –

Man
    what?

Electra
resting

Man
here?

Electra
I've walked miles today

Man
and you chose this spot?

Electra
it's a patch of ground, isn't it?

Man
then you are almost as stupid as you look
run girl
this isn't a place to rest
these graves are –
the men buried here

Electra
thieves and murderers, I know

Man
this is the most damned place in the whole land –

Electra
I know that too

Man
and still you stay?

He picks up the wine.

bit young for wine aren't you?

Electra
I'm older than I look

He hands it back.

Man
appeasing ghosts with wine, an outlawed art

Electra
  it's a picnic

Man
  oh I see, a picnic
  a girl like you, and a liquid picnic
  someone finds you here, they'll string you up
  why are you bringing a peace offering to this grave?

Electra
  the same reason you are standing here

Beat.

Man
  I am standing here telling you to go away
  I am standing here, saving your life

Electra
  fine

Man
  you were here yesterday
  with an old man

Electra
  a friend of mine

Man
  I saw you both, this isn't a picnic and this isn't you
    resting

Electra
  which is hers?
  I heard he was buried with a slave woman
  also murdered

Man
  you seem to know a lot about this

Electra
  my mother told me

189

Man
and who is your mother?

Electra
just a woman from the village

Beat.

their story is kind of famous

Electra puts flowers on the grave.

She pours a little of the wine.

can I sit for a second?

Man
you seem to have already

Electra sits on something.

Electra
oh

She finds what she is sitting on.

It's a wax image.

Man
don't touch that
they are laid out in a pattern

Electra
who is it of?

Man
the Queen
it brings bad luck to the Queen
I believe

Electra looks at it.

Electra
who would do such a thing?

Man
  plenty

Beat.

Electra
  poor Queen then

Man
  the most hated woman in the land
  her husband was loved and then she killed him so
  of course she is hated

Electra
  and no one has sympathy for her?

Man
  not many, she's a murderess
  do you?

Electra
  of course not

Beat.

  and you?

Man
  certainly not

Beat.

Electra
  it doesn't look like her anyway –

Man
  you've seen her then?

Electra
  hasn't everyone?

Man
 not for a while
 they say that she drinks herself stupid –

Electra
 not any more

Man
 you seem to know an awful lot about her?

Beat.

Electra
 people have got her wrong –
 she lost a girl

Man
 I know about that

Electra
 she killed the King because of the girl

Man
 you've been sent from the palace, haven't you?
 you have palace written all over you, who are you
  a serving girl?

Electra
 no

Man
 a spy then, to see what the enemies are saying?

Electra
 definitely not –

Man
 just like the Queen to send a girl
 get away from here or they'll kill you
 that man you were with, I recognised him
 he's the butcher
 he's from the palace too

Electra
    how did you recognise him if you have never been
        there?

Man
    don't try to trick me

Electra
    I know you who you are

Man
    unlikely

She pulls her cloak down.

Electra
    we have the same hair
    the same complexion

Man
    it's common around here

Electra
    we have the same eyes
    the same hands

Man
    who the fuck do you think you are?

Electra
    I am Electra, who are you?

Man
    Electra is just a baby

Electra
    I was
    then I grew up

Beat.

Man
    Electra?

Electra
    Orestes?

Beat.

    I've been waiting to see you
    all these months through all this
    no one talks about you
    I say what about my brother they say –

Orestes
    Orestes has gone
    no one can find him

Electra
    yes that's what they say

Orestes
    you should believe them

Electra
    I don't though

Orestes
    finish what you need to do then go.
    it's better that we don't talk

Electra
    why?

Beat.

Orestes
    we do have the same hair
    the same complexion

Electra
    it's like a mirror

Orestes
    go away, Electra, forget that you have seen me

Electra
    Mum isn't well
    the ghost is –

Orestes
    don't talk to me about the ghost
    the ghost?
    you think I don't know about the ghost –

Electra
    you too?

Orestes
    I heard these stories
    there are so many that wish her ill, I could hardly
        stop hearing these tales
    I would be in a town having a drink and someone
        would say
    it falls to you now
    the father is dead he can't avenge himself –
    ha ha I would go, back to my drink
    then someone else, it's up to you
    and someone else – just say the word
    shut up I would say
    I am not a hero
    I love my mother
    I had to move, keep moving
    wherever I went people would say they would build
        an army for me
    they were right behind me I just had to say the word
    I love my mother I said
    I love my mother
    I moved again
    I moved land, I crossed the sea
    I found a place, far from anywhere
    they didn't know me
    then it started
    just an itch at first

here on my feet
everyone gets itches I thought
I scratched a bit, thought nothing of it
then the other foot
good grief, that's itchy
it keep me awake a bit
it keeps me awake a lot, I hardly sleep now because
of the itches

Electra
maybe you need some cream –

Orestes
you think I haven't tried cream?
I haven't tried every cream?
then the behind the ears, it started as well
on my back
you have no idea how it itches –
I tore my clothes off

Electra
I don't understand

Orestes
you never knew him –
of course, I forget that
for you he was always away at war
but for me, when I was little he was there
he was always itchy
he had these scabs on his feet
it used to drive him crazy
you ask anyone
what was it that kept him awake during the nights
at Troy, fear of death, the pain of battle wounds?
no it was the itchy feet, and the back
if it was just the itches well okay but
he had a scar on his side where they took his appendix
out

I have still got my appendix
my appendix has not been taken out but look –

He lifts up his top.

He has a scar.

Electra
you sound like my mother

Orestes
he had two tattoos one on each arm
on one arm it said the name of the city on the other
the name of his wife

He pulls up his sleeves.

There are markings coming through.

Electra
what?

Orestes
you can almost read the words
I am turning into him
there is no other explanation
I have never had a tattoo
and I get these rages

Electra
dear Orestes

Orestes
no, it is not something that can be soothed by wine
or libation
the ghost also knows it falls to me
it falls to me, Electra
the ghost cannot avenge itself
so it falls to me

Electra
I have itchy feet too

I think you are making too much of this
so, we are his children, he has an affliction then
   it follows that we would –

Orestes
I have never had my appendix out

Electra lifts up her top.

She also has a scar.

She looks at Orestes.

Electra
I have never actually noticed
maybe I always had that

Orestes
it isn't just me
it is both of us!
you have it too

Electra
I love my mother

Orestes
so do I

Electra looks at her scar.

Electra
I don't believe in ghosts

Orestes
then what the fuck are you doing here?

Electra is frightened now.

I told you it was best that you hadn't seen me

Electra
I won't hurt her

Orestes
of course not, but the ghost won't stop until we do

Electra is alone. Back at the palace.

She takes off her clothes.

She looks at herself in the mirror.

She has a scar.

She has a rash on her arms.

She is itchy all over.

She looks at her hands.

Clytemnestra comes in.

Clytemnestra
there is a thing
I told them we shouldn't open the windows
the windows are no longer to be opened in the palace
    because of the wildlife. Outside.
Electra
don't open the windows and –

She goes over and shuts all the windows.

and you can't go out any more
no one must go out
you hear me, Electra?
it is important that you listen, that you do what you
    are told
we are in a new era now
you have to listen to me, we have to do what they
    tell us
we have to be very careful

Clytemnestra goes.

Electra is left with the mirror.

She looks again at her reflection.

She is really itchy.

She starts to scratch.

Electra
    stop

She shouts into the mirror.

    stop stop this

She itches all over.

She smashes the mirror.

SCENE TEN

Electra puts some clothes on.

She goes in to find the King.

The King is talking to the Doctor.

Aegisthus
    I'm busy
    can't you see I am busy?
    you walked straight in, you didn't knock

Electra
    I need to talk to you –

Aegisthus
    later
    or no, not later, never
    do go on, doctor

The Doctor takes a breath to go on but Electra hasn't left.

Aegisthus looks up at her.

Aegisthus
can't you hear properly?
shall I get the doctor to check your ears while he is here

Electra
I want to be sent away
I don't mean just now I mean properly
I want to be sent away far away

That stops the King, he speaks to the Doctor.

Aegisthus
excuse me for a minute

Doctor
of course

The Doctor retreats a bit.

The King speaks to Electra.

Aegisthus
why would you ask to be sent away?

Electra
Orestes was sent to school when he was my age

Aegisthus
Orestes was a boy

Electra
there are schools for girls
I want to go to school

Aegisthus
why on earth out of the blue are you asking to be
    sent away?

Electra
I thought you'd be pleased

Aegisthus
I might be

        if I trusted you
        if I didn't think that every single thing you do isn't
            full of poison

Electra
        I need an education
        at some point I need to learn something

Aegisthus
        you hate me
        everything you have done since I have been here has
            been spiteful, has been to drive a wedge between
            me and your mother

Electra
        so send me away

Aegisthus
        this will be some trick
        maybe the whole sleep thing was a trick by you
        I see it now
        somehow you think it will reflect on me
        you get sent away and the Queen blames me
        ah yes that is your game
        true to form poison
        doctor, have you any way of treating a poisonous girl?

Electra
        there is nothing wrong with me

Aegisthus
        then stay out of my way.
        keep your evil plans to yourself
        no, Electra.
        you asked to go so you must stay
        you must stay here.
        you will stay here and watch your mother become mine
        if that's what you are trying to avoid, too bad
        she'll turn away from you and turn towards me

that's the right and proper way of these things.
you watch

SCENE ELEVEN

Electra is vomiting.

No one comes.

She keeps vomiting.

The Butcher eventually comes.

Butcher
  oh God

He gets a bucket.

  when did this start?

She retches again.

  its okay, don't speak.
  maybe you should get back to bed –

Again Electra is sick.

  it's okay sweetheart
  its just a fever or perhaps some bug.
  can I have some help in here?

No one answers.

He rubs her back.

  or something disagreed with you, maybe you ate
      something –
  let's get you back to bed

She seems resistant.

  come on, if you are sick it's better to be in bed

The serving woman, Celia, comes in.

Celia
she'll wake everyone

Butcher
help me then

Celia
I'm just saying then there'll be all hell to pay
if the King wakes up

Butcher
wake her mother

Electra is sick again.

Electra
no, not the Queen

Butcher
maybe you got cold today, maybe you picked up a chill

Clytemnestra comes in.

Clytemnestra
what's wrong with her?

Butcher
she isn't well

Clytemnestra
the smell?
can she smell it too?

Celia
we think she needs her mother

Clytemnestra
no, not me
how can I help when I'm like this?
bring a little water, would you
give the girl some water

Butcher
of course

The Butcher goes to get some water.

Electra retches again.

Clytemnestra is torn whether to go to help her.

Clytemnestra
it's okay, it's okay
you'll be okay
you'll be okay in a bit
oh God

She starts to pull away.

another bucket

Celia
what is it?

Clytemnestra
there are flies in the vomit

Celia
no

Clytemnestra
yes, she is heaving up insects
they are coming out of her mouth

Celia
just some in the bucket perhaps

Clytemnestra
she is turning rotten, I can see it

Celia
nonsense

Clytemnestra
and you, you have dropped something
there must you always be dropping something

Electra is sick again.

everyone everyone is always dropping something
why can people not stop dropping things?

Clytemnestra runs off.

The Butcher comes back holding the bucket.

Celia is there too.

Electra
Mum?

Clytemnestra has gone.

SCENE TWELVE

Electra and Orestes are outside. Electra is sitting on the grass.

Electra
why haven't you left then?

Orestes
my feet won't take me
simple as that
every day I think I will walk to the next city, I will
   go in that direction, and every night

Electra
that's ridiculous

Orestes
why haven't you left?

Electra
the King won't let me

Beat.

we'll have to leave together.
we could go in the middle of the night
I could pack a bag –

Orestes
  and go where?

Electra
  anywhere

Orestes
  we'll come back

Electra
  we could try not to
  we have to try not to

Orestes
  and scratch for the rest of our lives?

Electra
  what alternative is there?

Orestes
  you know what the alternative is –

Electra
  ha ha

Orestes
  why are you so loyal to her?

Electra
  this isn't about loyalty
  don't be absurd, I love her
  she's troubled but she –

Orestes
  it's okay for you, you still sleep
  I haven't slept for three weeks
  you wait
  in a few weeks you would do anything
  there is a dance, the doctors call it a dance when
      you are so itchy you go mad
  you'll scratch yourself against any tree
  people die trying to get rid of an itch

there are times when I want to take my own skin
    off with a knife
pour boiling water, anything to make it stop

Beat.

Electra
    this is a sort of madness
    why is everyone mad?

Orestes
    she has convinced you that everything she did, she
        did out of love
    that she is this perfect woman –

Electra
    she is

Orestes
    then why does half the country hate her?
    have you thought about that?

Electra
    there are rumours spread –
    yes okay

Orestes
    she killed in cold blood –

Electra
    so did he

Orestes
    he thought it was a sex game
    she killed him with an erection

Beat.

Electra
    this is their fight
    I don't want to hear about that

Orestes
I'll tell you something about the butcher
I'll tell you something about the pair of them

Electra
if this is more lies

Orestes
I met someone who used to work at the palace
someone who fled that night, most people fled that
    night

Electra
the butcher is a good person

Orestes
of course he is

Electra
he put me to bed, I heard the tale

Orestes
there is a missing patch of that evening
after he cleaned the flagstones
after he put you to bed
no one could find him

Electra
so?

Orestes
and no one could find our mother after

Electra
I know where they were

Orestes
you heard the tale then?

Electra
I know they were with the body
he carried the body

Orestes
but that isn't all

Electra
he brought it out to the field

Orestes
he is a butcher
why did she go to the butcher?

Beat.

why did she go to the butcher that night?

Beat.

you know nothing, Electra, you know nothing about
this world

Electra
I don't want to hear

Orestes
you have to hear
yes this is their fight, but it is also ours
the ghost is making it ours
in the old folk-lore, like they believe in the butcher's
town
there is a saying
you want to disempower a ghost
if someone has been murdered say, and you are
worried
you do something to the body

Electra
I don't believe this –

Orestes
why is the butcher so close to her?
they have secrets you know that

Electra
stop

Orestes
you want to disempower a ghost, you take a sharp
  knife
let's say a butcher's knife and before you bury the body
you cut off the penis
they took off his penis

Electra
how do you know?

Orestes
you want to dig him up, check?
they took off his penis and they stuck it under his arm
for all of heaven to laugh at
for him forever to be mocked
you ask anyone
they dug up his body, the men loyal to him
they found his fucking penis under his arm
that is why she is so hated
she used a kind of witchcraft
now I am not saying that she wasn't justified in what
  she did
that there wasn't some sense in which
and our sister after all –
but if she was so certain that she was right
why do that to him, he was already dead?
why cut off his penis?
why stick it under his arm?

Electra sits up.

Electra
that's grotesque
I don't believe you, you fill my head with this stuff

Orestes
  she doesn't love you
  she doesn't love you
  she can't love anyone but herself
  it has always been that way

Electra
  stop it

Orestes
  you want me to tell you the tales of when you were
    smaller?
  she was drunk most of your life
  she hardly knew you were there

Electra
  she was troubled

Orestes
  she has always been troubled
  when I was a child, before Iphigenia, she was the same
  she is a distracted woman, part of the same line
  concerned with herself

Electra
  I won't kill her

Orestes
  but let me

Electra
  Orestes I can't even believe

Orestes
  I can't live like this
  I am in torment
  give me permission
  you and I are the only ones left

Beat.

Electra
there is no point asking me, you know what I will say
this is just talk anyway, you

Orestes
then you'll keep me in torment

Beat.

Electra
she loves you

Orestes
she is afraid of me

Electra
no

Orestes
of course she is, she will have heard the rumours,
that I am the one to avenge

Electra
she misses you

Orestes
I bet she never even speaks of me
have you ever heard her bring up my name?
she would like to hear the news that I am dead
that would make her day
if I am dead there is no threat from the ghost
we both know that

Electra
you are so wrong

Orestes
I wish I was

Electra
let's see then

Orestes
what?

Electra
let's tell her you are dead
see what she does

Orestes
she won't weep

Electra
you'll see
she loves you.

Orestes
and if she doesn't?

Electra
if she doesn't weep?

Orestes
yes

Electra
impossible
she loves her children more than herself, everything
she does she does for them
she says that all the time

Orestes
if she doesn't weep?

Electra
then yes
I'll release you

SCENE THIRTEEN

Electra is in the dining room.

She is setting the scene. Making sure everything is ready.

214

She puts a tablecloth on the table.

The Butcher comes in. He takes the cloth from her.

Butcher
I'll do that

Electra
no its okay
I can do it

Beat.

She sets the cloth.

He starts to move a chair.

I can do that too

He stops.

Butcher
is there anything you want from me?

Electra
not much

Beat.

Butcher
I don't see you now
you used to come to the kitchen and have some milk

Electra
I did once

Butcher
we used to speak sometimes

Beat.

when I pass you in the corridor –

Electra
I don't have much time

Butcher
you are changed

Electra
do you think you should talk to me like that?

Beat.

Butcher
I . . .

Electra
I am the one with the title here
you are the butcher

Butcher
apologies, miss

He looks at her.

Electra
go on
you can go

He walks out.

Electra stops. She feels bad.

She takes a deep breath.

She goes to a curtain. Orestes is there, behind it.

Orestes
that was sharp

Electra
he cut off my father's dick, what am I supposed to say?
shush someone is coming

Orestes pulls back the curtain.

Electra sits down.

Then changes her mind, stands up.

Smoothes her dress down.

Feels nervous.

Clytemnestra comes in.

Clytemnestra
I heard there was some news

Electra
can you sit down

Clytemnestra
it's news that I need to sit down for?

Electra
where's the King?

Clytemnestra
do we need him here too?

Electra
how are the flies today?

Clytemnestra
not good.
worse but the windows are shut

Electra
what's that smell?

Clytemnestra
you smell it too

Electra
you used to smell like that
on your breath

Clytemnestra
get away

Electra
  are you drinking?

Clytemnestra
  you told me there was news

Beat.

Electra
  Orestes is dead

Beat.

Clytemnestra
  what?

Electra
  Orestes is dead.
  Mum, I'm so sorry

Clytemnestra
  how?

Electra
  I met a man and a woman on the road

Clytemnestra
  you went out?

Electra
  for a short time only

Clytemnestra
  what man what woman?

Electra
  they were on their way to us
  he was on a ship, returning home I think
  he had heard about you being asleep
  he was coming back to see you

Clytemnestra
  how did he die?

Electra
he drowned

Beat.

they had a letter explaining what happened
I . . .

She hands her mother a letter.

Clytemnestra
you read it?

Electra
they said it concerned my brother
I thought I could read it, yes I'm sorry –

The Queen reads the letter.

Clytemnestra
and it's true?
it's definite?

Electra
of course it's true

Clytemnestra
where is this man and this woman?

Electra
on the road, we could catch them probably if we –

The Queen looks at the letter again.

Clytemnestra
can you call the butcher, the smell is worse
tell him to bring something to take it away
tell the butcher to come quick

She stands up.

Clytemnestra
oh goodness
oh gods

I . . .
the flies will break through the window

She looks a little dizzy.

Electra
    are you okay?

Clytemnestra
    my Orestes, my only boy
    this can't be
    my little one
    I . . .
    could you bring me some water?
    there has been so much death in this house
    and get the butcher

Electra pours her some water.

Clytemnestra sits down and drinks it.

    add something to it, would you
    this isn't the time for your disapproval
    I need a drink, my son is dead –
    I had a dream
    a terrifying dream, a dream so bad I didn't want to
        wake up
    I dreamt about my Orestes
    funny I dreamt about him last night
    as a little baby –
    he was such a lovely baby
    not my first of course but
    I dreamt he was once again in my arms, his red hair
        just like it was the day he was born
    a crease across his nose
    and I was feeding him
    you'll know the joy of feeding a child one day, Electra
    the close softness
    and then as I stroked his little head

I dropped the baby
I dropped him on the floor and instead of it smashing
    or crying or
I bent to pick it up
I was scrabbling around trying to pick him up
it turned into a snake and hissed at me
it was a snake I'd had drinking at my breast
not my baby at all
a snake that bit me

She drinks the water.

and now he's dead
according to this letter
I asked a seer
he said it was easy to interpret
Orestes would kill me
Orestes was the snake
the flies knew it
I knew it
the gods knew it
Orestes would kill me

She puts the glass back down.

the gods will forgive me I have been frightened yes
I know I am damned
but to be killed by your son

She takes the bottle from the table. Pours it into her glass.

and now you tell me he is drowned.
fuck's sake I need a drink will someone get me
    something

Aegisthus comes into the room.

Aegisthus
what was so urgent I had to be –

Clytemnestra
my son is dead
Orestes, drowned

Aegisthus
how?

Clytemnestra
returning home it seems
gone, done not far from here

Aegisthus looks to Electra.

a letter came

He takes the letter.

Electra
I'm sorry

Aegisthus starts to read the letter.

Clytemnestra
yes so am I.
very sorry
very very sorry
I'm sorry for you, Electra too, you never knew him

Aegisthus
where were these people?

Clytemnestra
out on the road

Aegisthus
this is poison
this is some trick

Clytemnestra
no, I can feel it
he is dead

Aegisthus
well then let's find them, these people that brought
the news

The Butcher comes in.

Butcher
madam, you called
I have made something to clear the smell

Clytemnestra
the smell?

Butcher
you wanted me to –

She stands up.

Clytemnestra
that's the most surprising thing
the smell has gone

She breathes in.

it's gone
I can't smell anything

The Butcher sniffs.

and the headache –

She laughs.

open the windows, let the outside in
bring me something to celebrate

Electra
you must be sad though? your son

Clytemnestra
yes

Electra
very sad?
maybe you will weep?

Clytemnestra
yes it is sad but
he was young, he had never done anything bad in
   his life
the gods will look on him favourably
whereas I –
if I were to have died
I would have been damned

She laughs.

the seer got it wrong
I am not going to die

She kisses Electra.

I think we should celebrate that shouldn't we?
with a drink

She kisses Aegisthus.

Orestes is dead
I am not going to die

Aegisthus kisses her back.

Aegisthus
finally

Clytemnestra
yes finally

She kisses him again.

She laughs.

we can get back to where we should have been.
bring a fucking drink. Let's have a party

Aegisthus grabs her around the waist and carries her off.
She squeals.

SCENE FOURTEEN

Orestes and Electra are left in the room.

There is a kind of stunned silence between them.

Orestes

    we still don't need to do it

    we can spend eternity tormented

    it is a suggestion

    not a command

    the ghost is urging us

    we have free will

    what are you doing?

Electra

    I'm listening.

    I'm listening to what they are saying as he carries

        her to bed.

Orestes

    come away

Beat.

Electra

    I always knew she wasn't exactly

    well no one is perfect

    is anyone perfect?

    I knew she would forget me sometimes

    and sometimes she would say she would come up

        and then wouldn't

    or even sometimes she wouldn't see me at all for days

    leave me waiting

    and when she was drinking of course

    but I always thought

    that somewhere

    sometime

    the next time

    deep down that really

Orestes
we don't have to do this

Electra
you were right about her

Orestes
I think we should think about

Electra
rip down the walls
see what they are doing in there

Orestes
it is natural

Electra
you should have stood at the wall and listened to
what they said as they walked away
you have to have good ears if you want to know
what goes on in here
he knew the letter was false, I could see that
he knew that there was no woman and no man on
the road
you see he didn't send anyone to find them
he's clever, he knew
he says I am full of poison, maybe I am

Orestes
what did he say?

Electra
he told her
he said, Orestes isn't dead this is a false report

Orestes
I didn't hear that

Electra
but I did
you didn't stand where I stood

Orestes
and what did she say?

Electra
she said the thing that damns her most of all –
she said, find him then and kill him

Beat.

Electra looks at Orestes.

she said find him then and kill him –
kill my son

Orestes
you misheard –

Electra
I didn't.
you were right about her.
you were right, how can you say I misheard?
you were right

Clytemnestra comes in, half dressed, to get the bottle.

Clytemnestra
oh, I am sorry, Electra, I didn't realise –

Aegisthus' voice off.

Aegisthus
hurry, darling

Clytemnestra
I will, I just
who's this?

Orestes gets out a knife.

Orestes
I'm your son, mother

Clytemnestra
but –

227

Orestes
it's been so long you don't even recognise me

Clytemnestra
of course I recognise you –
Aegisthus!

Orestes
don't call for anyone

Clytemnestra
now wait a minute, don't come near me
put that away

Orestes
this is not from me, this is from my father

Clytemnestra
Orestes, no –

She drops the bottle she is holding.

It smashes.

Orestes grabs his mother, gets her into a hold.

He doesn't kill her straight away, though – hesitates, panics.

you don't have the nerve,
you always were a timid boy
you can't do this

Orestes
don't push me

Clytemnestra
do it then

Orestes
I . . .

He drops the knife.

Clytemnestra
    you can't kill your mother
    you see?
    it's against the law of nature

Electra comes over.

She picks up the knife.

    tell him, Electra
    there's no one that loves you more than a mother
    no one that loves her children more than a mother
        does

Electra puts the knife into Clytemnestra.

Clytemnestra falls.

She is screaming.

Orestes
    finish her, you only half did it

Electra
    you do it

Orestes
    I can't

Electra puts the knife into her again. Cold-blooded.

The screaming stops.

Aegisthus comes in, half dressed.

Aegisthus
    oh God
    what the hell – guards
    you're surrounded

Orestes
    by who?

Aegisthus
    you won't get away with this

Orestes
    everyone hates you more than we do

He grabs Aegisthus, they fight.

Aegisthus
    someone will stop you, someone will
    you think you have strength

Orestes kills him swiftly. He breaks his neck.

Aegisthus falls on to the floor.

Silence.

Orestes and Electra look at what they have done.

They are covered in blood.

They look at each other.

Orestes
    okay?

Electra
    yes, okay

Orestes
    sure?

Electra
    sure

The Butcher comes running in.

Butcher
    what's the noise?
    what's going on, what is going on here?

He sees the two bodies.

    what?
    what have you done?

oh hell.
what have you done?

Celia is behind him.

She sees the bodies too, and puts her hand to her face.

Electra
there is nothing here for you, please leave us

The Butcher runs to the Queen.

Orestes takes the knife from Electra. He uses the tablecloth to wipe it.

Butcher
the doctor, someone call the doctor!

Electra
there is no one here –
who will hear you?

Butcher
what have you done, you evil girl?

Celia pulls him away from the Queen's body.

Celia
she's dead
they both are
you have to come away

Butcher
but these two –

Celia
nothing can be done
this time you have to run

Butcher
Electra, this isn't you

Celia
the curse on this house is too much
you warned me that the curse here –

Butcher
Electra –

Celia
you can't wash the flagstones again, try to solve it
you can't keep washing the flagstones
not again

Butcher
Electra – look at me

Celia
come with me now

She pulls him away.

come on, its time to leave this

Celia and the Butcher go.

Orestes and Electra are left.

Orestes wipes the blood from Electra's face.

Carefully. Tenderly.

Orestes
the curse is broken

Electra
the itch?

Orestes
gone
everything that was done between them
it's over now

Electra
yes

Orestes
we're free then? Aren't we?
we can do what we want with our lives
live differently
we'll bury them
we will put all three in a proper grave
it finishes here
the woman was right this has been a curse
a curse that goes back as long as either of us can
remember but now

Electra's hand starts to shake.

what is that with your hand?

Electra
I don't know, it –

Orestes
just the shock

Electra
yes

Orestes
let's go to the kitchen and get you something sweet
everyone will have gone, we'll have the place to
ourselves

Her hand shakes even more.

what is it?

Electra
I don't know

She looks at her arms, her legs.

She can't control it.

what's happening to me?

Orestes tries to hold her.

233

Orestes
    it'll be okay, just try to take some deep breaths

Electra
    help me

The shakes take over her whole body.

Then she falls to the floor. This is a full blown seizure.

Orestes
    stop if you can, Electra
    Electra
    deep breaths

Orestes calls out to anyone that will listen.

    help
    out there
    someone help
    someone help my sister
    someone help my sister please

Electra continues to shake.

    SOMEONE HELP MY SISTER

PART THREE
ELECTRA AND HER SHADOW

Characters

Electra
Clytemnestra
Agamemnon
Orestes
Chorus
Audrey
Jordan
Michael
Megan
Owen
Ian
Iphigenia

SCENE ONE

Electra is holding the knife exactly the same as at the end of the previous play.

She is shaking.

She is otherwise alone on stage.

Electra
Orestes?
Orestes are you there?
don't piss about –
Orestes?
is that you?
I can hear you

She moves around the stage with the knife.

if you're playing a game
then fuck off, fuck off with your teasing.

There is a sniffing.

A snuffling, an odd sort of noise. Unsettling. It's not even clear where it comes from.

this isn't funny
don't scare me

Faceless forms seem to be in the shadows, or is it her imagination?

There is a chill, a wind.

stop it, Orestes.

She looks around.

Electra
  Orestes. Stop it.
  stop it.

She is in the middle of a wood.

She looks around.

Clytemnestra is sitting in a chair. Blood all down her.

Clytemnestra
  hell my darling
  I could see your mouth moving to ask the question
  hell is the answer

Electra
  that can't be you –

Clytemnestra
  yes me

Electra looks around.

Electra
  but, how can it be? I just

Clytemnestra
  put a knife through me?
  well done but now –

Electra
  you're alive?

Clytemnestra
  sadly not
  very dead and this place . . .

Electra
  where's Orestes?

Clytemnestra
  gone
  the palace, gone

everything you know, gone
you know of all my kids I expected this least from you
you were my little biddable poppet

Electra
stay away from me –

Clytemnestra
I can't even touch you
you might not like being here but look, Electra
at least look at me

Electra
I'm dreaming, I know I'm dreaming

Clytemnestra
if you wish

Electra
get back

Electra backs away.

Clytemnestra
oh sweetheart there is a lot worse to come
you have unleashed something

Electra
what do you mean?

Clytemnestra
I don't know but can't you hear them?
scratching, sniffing
in the dark when you have your eyes shut
moving about in the undergrowth

Electra
I'm not scared

Clytemnestra
you should be
you should be very very scared

you killed your mother. You foolish girl
all hell is coming for you now
you had better run

The sound returns, terrible now. And terrifying.

All around. Electra doesn't know which way to turn.

*The lights change. Electra is on a snow-covered
mountain.*

Electra
oh God

*Her father is standing beside her. She doesn't see him at
first.*

Agamemnon
Electra

Electra
please, Mum, if that's you

Agamemnon
my baby

Electra
what?

Agamemnon
it's me, your father

Electra looks at him for the first time.

Electra
my father's dead

Agamemnon
yes okay, but here to help you
you have to fight this, you can't let them destroy you

Electra
what are they?

Agamemnon
　I don't know but your mother is behind it
　take everything I have, all the power I had
　you just have to find their weakness
　if they are sent by your mother then they'll have
　　a weakness
　arm yourself, find every weapon you can
　think like a soldier you have to fight back

Electra hears the wind again.

Electra
　I don't even know which direction they are coming
　　from

Agamemnon
　it's the blood on your hands
　that's what is bringing them

She looks down.

She wipes her hands.

Electra
　there's blood on us both

Agamemnon
　but my crimes do not insult them like yours

Electra
　I can't fight

Agamemnon
　then keep the window shut
　don't let them in
　if you can't fight them, keep them out

Electra
　what window?

The noise starts to come back.

　DAD?

She looks about her.

Agamemnon
run, Electra

Electra
DAD?

Agamemnon
run

He has gone.

She is on the beach.

She sits up.

Electra
where now?

Orestes
don't ask

Electra
Orestes? Thank goodness
we have to get out of here

Orestes
I wish it was different –

Electra
what was different?

Orestes
I am not with you any more

Electra
yes, you were in the palace beside me
something terrible is after us

Orestes
I was yes, right by your side
but then –

Electra
no don't tell me

Orestes
we were in the dining room

Electra
on the floor

Orestes
you started shaking
this terrible shaking,
Electra, I was scared
forgive me please, when I saw what had happened
   to you

Electra
forgive you?

Orestes
I went into a panic –
I knew the gods were angry

Electra
there are no gods

Orestes
okay, creatures older than the gods even
these terrors and spirits
I heard them
I ran out into the field and with a piece of rope –

Electra
no

Orestes
we broke some rule
I'm sorry, Electra
when I saw them coming

Electra
we're together, we're together in this

Orestes

    not any more
    it was your hand holding the knife
    it's you they want

Electra

    you left me

Orestes

    I'm no use to you, I never was any use

Electra

    so be of use now, how do I face this?

Orestes

    I don't know what the answer is
    I think you should run

Electra

    where to?

Orestes

    who knows?
    a place they won't find you

Electra

    and where is that?
    where the hell is that?
    where do I run?

The Chorus come on to the stage.

They sing a song. A song about a woman who runs around the whole world. A woman who never stops running. It's a sort of lullaby, but then gets fucked up. One of them keeps fucking it up. The Chorus get cross with each other. Clytemnestra says she knows this one and joins in. She picks up the story about the woman that ran, it has become scatological. She forgets the rhyme that goes at the end of it. Agamemnon and Orestes join in with the chorus. They take a turn. They seem more modern now. Microphones and guitars. One of them is still trying to keep it sweet. What hope for a good ending is there? Does anyone know?

Electra even has a solo spot.

When it comes to her verse, the answer to 'is there any hope of a happy ending', she has the microphone. She answers.

Electra
none at all

SCENE TWO

Audrey enters carrying a whole load of files.

She goes over to the filing cabinet. She puts the files in the filing cabinet.

She speaks to a Chorus member that is in her way.

Audrey
you shouldn't be here
and I know you are listening because your hand
    twitches when you are off in a dwarm
Jordan, should you be here?

Jordan looks confused.

Jordan
I think I . . .

Audrey
exactly.
back out the door, along the corridor
go and sit in the day room
do you want me to ring for the nurse?

She puts the files back, ignoring him.

He still stands there.

She takes down a sweetie jar.

Audrey
alright, one. Then back to your ward

She opens the jar, she gives him a sweet.

Jordan sucks on it and goes out.

As he goes he passes Michael on the way in.

Michael
I thought you didn't do that any more –

Audrey
it's Jordan

Michael
new paper out, shouldn't reward

Audrey
again, it's Jordan

Michael
they're all somebody

Audrey
sweet tooth

Michael
you brought magazines in for Carol
don't tell me, it's Carol
and special pyjamas for Ted

Audrey
what can I say?
busted.

Beat.

life is miserable enough, isn't it?
the odd sweet

Michael
quite, but who is going to do that when you have gone?

248

Audrey
  if you've come to try and talk me out of going –

Michael
  heaven forfend. I know when a mind is made up

Audrey moves over to a second cabinet and starts sorting stuff.

Audrey
  could you move over actually? I have to get to that
    drawer

Michael
  sorry. Are you packing case notes already?

Audrey
  I've got to make a start
  you wouldn't believe the amount of crap I have
    accrued
  if it was just the case notes

He is still a bit in the way.

  not in a clinic?

Michael
  finished early

Audrey
  oh.

He is completely in the way. He moves off slightly.

Michael
  I'll miss you

Audrey
  I know
  I'll miss you too
  this building though I won't miss
  apparently I get a view right across the river in Ohio

Michael
do you want a drink?

Audrey
I've got patients to see

Michael
alright. Later
you know you've got your window open

Audrey
oh?

Michael
shall I shut it?

Audrey
I don't remember opening it

Michael
well it's open now
easy fixed

He shuts it.

Audrey looks at the window.

Audrey
perhaps Jordan opened it

She goes over and makes sure it is shut.

Michael
have a drink with me
you are a bloody good psychiatrist, you can do it on
half a glass of sherry

Audrey
you are a bad influence

Michael
busted

Audrey gets a bottle of sherry out of a filing cabinet.

She pours them both a glass.

saw you saw some of your old patients again yesterday

Audrey
I put some of them down for my clinic, yes

Michael
how did it go?

Audrey
fine, I had space

Michael
okay

Audrey
why are you asking?

Michael
no reason

Audrey
you never normally ask about my clinics

Michael
we never normally have a drink in the afternoon
is there a problem with that?

Audrey
the drink or the asking?

Beat.

Michael
I was just surprised that is all
to see you go back to your old list

Audrey
I wanted to say goodbye to this place
to them

Michael
other people look after that ward now

Audrey
so there is a problem –

Michael
Audrey no
you're a grown-up
you're a bloody good psychiatrist as I said

Beat.

Audrey
there are some loose ends

Michael
be careful

Audrey
you cured me

Michael
I know I did

Beat.

Audrey
I'm only here for another three weeks
yes, there is a kind of black mark
most people respond to something, in the end
or they just get so much worse that they disappear
    and the body gives up
but

Michael
some people we can't help

Audrey
I am only here for another three weeks
is there such a danger in trying?

Michael
your window is open again

Audrey
what?

She looks.

    no it isn't

Michael
    but you jumped. You looked in alarm

Audrey
    for God's sake

Michael
    I was the person who went through it with you
    you're jumpy

Audrey
    the window opened today because, I don't know why
        the window was open
    maybe I opened it and I forgot
    or Jordan or
    what the fuck are you doing playing games with me?

Michael
    I'm sorry you are reacting like this

Audrey
    she was a patient of mine for a long time
    I have three weeks before I go.
    if I can do something
    stop looking at the fucking window

Michael
    I've made you cross

Audrey
    damn right you have

Beat.

He hands his glass back to her.

Michael
    I'm sorry

she and you weren't the same
your cases are different

Audrey
I know.

Michael
enjoy the last three weeks here, Audrey.
you're such a valuable member of our team
so loved
don't let her drag you back to somewhere

Audrey
how could she?

Michael
indeed.
how could she?

A psychiatric nurse, Megan, comes in.

Megan
that's your clinic starting, Audrey

Audrey
thank you

Megan
some have been waiting a little while, what shall I tell
them?

Audrey
I'm coming

Audrey picks up some files and walks out in a rush.

Megan is left with Michael. She sees the glasses of sherry.

Megan
didn't know this was a party –

Michael
it wasn't

SCENE THREE

Electra sits in a chair.

Audrey stands a little way off.

Electra
you stopped seeing me

Audrey
doctors move on, we see a patient for a while, we feel
we aren't getting anywhere, we –

Electra
you passed me on

Beat.

Audrey
it became complicated

Electra
so why are you back?

Audrey
I . . .
you're a curiosity around here
you don't fit, you know that
most of the patients, well there is a thing that goes
with mental illness –

Electra
I'm not mentally ill

Audrey
that isn't actually the complication, many people with
symptoms say that but you – most people's
symptoms can be medicated in the end, the doses
might get high and they get sleepy but the psychosis

255

is suppressed.
you – we give higher and higher doses of medication,
neither does it have any effect nor does it appear
to sedate you

Electra
that is because it isn't psychosis

Audrey
of course

Electra
if it was psychosis I would respond

Audrey
indeed
not psychosis then, a sort of paranoia, a high state
of anxiety and terror that nothing seems to relieve

Electra
I am cursed

Audrey
and you know I have heard your explanation

Electra
but you don't believe it

Audrey
we are here to explore the connection between the
psyche and the body, the physical manifestations of
your belief that you are being hunted

Electra
I am

Audrey
and I promise we will explore that

Electra
hell will get me one day.

Audrey
not if I can help it

Electra
>the window isn't even shut properly. You haven't put the bolt across. The door could swing open at any second
>there are cracks in the floorboards. There is a vent through which anything could come

Audrey stands up.

Audrey
>I can put a bolt across the window
>I can do whatever I can to make you feel safe

Electra
>I never feel safe

Audrey looks at the vent.

Audrey
>I hadn't noticed the vent

Electra
>and there is an old chimney behind that wall

Audrey stands on a chair.

Audrey
>I'll ask them to look into that

Electra
>the nurses don't check under the beds properly.
>there are little holes in the skirting boards

Audrey
>we can fill the holes

Electra
>if you restrain me I can't even run

Audrey
>you were running for years
>it did you no good

Electra
  just let me go

She pulls at the restraints.

  please

Audrey
  your clothes had fallen away
  you were so dehydrated you were nearly dead

Electra
  what else is there to do?

Beat.

Electra pulls again at the ties holding her.

Audrey
  you know if you took responsibility for what you did,
    then release might be –

Electra
  I have taken responsibility

Audrey
  worked through your remorse

Electra
  how can I be remorseful for something I was supposed
    to do?

Audrey
  you understand you killed your mother

Electra
  of course I do
  but she deserved to die

Audrey rubs her face in her hands.

Audrey
  I think this is where you get blocked
  I think this is the root of it all

Electra

it wasn't just a voice in my head, it wasn't just a
feeling of compulsion
she was going to kill my brother

Audrey

what, literally, in front of you?

Electra

she killed my father, she is capable of anything

Audrey

you understand the theories of how the brain works,
don't you? You've read the books I lent you

Electra

she sent them to hunt me
they are a curse from her

Audrey

she is dead

Electra

yes but even dead –
you watching now, Mum, you enjoying this?

Audrey

there is this fixation on your mother

Electra

because she's enjoying it, and it isn't fair

There is a noise.

Audrey

that is just the air conditioning
no need for your alarm, it's a new system

She stands up, looks at the vent.

I'll get someone to check it

She comes back down, sits on the chair.

259

Electra
    you can't take your eye off the little spaces, they can
        crawl through anything, wherever there is a gap
    I ask my father, there must be someone I can appeal to?
    even hell must have some sort of reason.

Audrey
    and what does he say?

Electra
    my father is useless
    he says I should wrap a piece of ribbon around my
        wrist
    and then there is my brother

Audrey
    you see all your family?

Electra
    I see everyone
    the whole household, pretty much everywhere

Beat.

Audrey looks at her.

    you are making a note

Audrey
    I am thinking.

Electra
    you'll say something clever and this will all be over?

Audrey
    I doubt it

Electra
    then what's the point?

Beat.

Audrey
    you're an intelligent person, Electra

you know you're in a permanent state of terror and
      paranoia
brought on by your crime
that is the diagnosis, the worst anyone has even seen
and distressing of course
but tell me
if they are so powerful is a window enough? A door,
      a bolt, the nurse checking the spaces?

Electra

why do you say that?

Audrey

put it another way, they want you
they are coming for you
you say you are being hunted

Electra

they do come in sometimes
they come in and play sometimes

Audrey

tell me about that

Electra

they are the spirit of the torture chamber
the executioner's knife
there is no pain like it
so painful that you forget who you are
and just when I can bear no more, and I am crying out,
they whisper or laugh in my ear
they say they will be back another day and then it will
      be worse

Beat.

Audrey

I didn't realise they could talk?

Electra

I can hear what they are saying, yes

Beat.

Audrey
when we have these episodes on tape, it looks like you bruise yourself

Electra
they bruise me

Audrey
you can see why it is difficult for us to understand

Electra
they bite and kick and rip then leave me healed so they can do it again

Audrey
I see

Beat.

Electra
I have a message actually

Beat.

the message is for you

Audrey
okay

Electra
when they came the time before, they whispered something

Audrey
what did they whisper?

Electra
they whispered that they are coming for you too

Beat.

Audrey
right, I see

Electra
they've been hunting for you as well
you don't have to believe me

Audrey
are you trying to scare me too, so we can sit in the
same place?

Electra
I'm just passing on a message

Audrey
from them?

Electra
yes from them

Audrey
well, thank you for the message

Electra
I think you knew that already

Audrey
if they come for me, I will deal with it.

Beat.

Electra
you had better be prepared

Audrey
I will be

Electra
they are no fun

Beat.

is it my time?

Audrey
yes
that is your time
thank you Electra
I'll get a nurse to take you back

SCENE FOUR

Audrey goes in to see Michael in his office.

Michael
long day?

Audrey
aren't they all?

Michael
I'm up to my ears in it, Lesley W's back

Audrey
I thought she was discharged –

Michael
well, she returned
could you sign this?
right royal mess, we shouldn't have discharged her
    in the community's view
read it first

Audrey
do I want to?

Michael
no, probably not
you're out of here after all.
sign if you could

Audrey signs.

what did you want?

Audrey
not sure

Michael
you going for a run?

Audrey
I was thinking about it, how can you tell?

Michael
you're holding your trainers

Audrey looks down.

Audrey
oh
need to clear my head
running is good for that

Michael
wish I was as disciplined, could do with getting rid
    of some of this spare –

Audrey
hallucinations, gremlins, what are they?

Michael
what?

Audrey
what sort of thing?

Michael
what sort of thing are hallucinations?

Audrey
yes

Michael
sensory reworkings often

Audrey
of what?

Michael
past experiences
memories, desires
emotions
dreams sometimes

Audrey
anything else?

Michael
internal states, you know the range is enormous
you just about wrote the book on these things, why
are you asking me?

Audrey
I'm just checking

She puts her shoes on.

internal states absolutely. Guilt being one of the most
painful to the ego
that we didn't act as we wished we had, because it
contradicts who we think we should be, who we are
it's an irritant
or we feel we were wronged, that we shouldn't be
blamed
that the universe is unjust
and that is always it, there is never anything else

Michael
is everything okay?

Audrey
of course it is

She does her shoelaces up.

damn

The lace has snapped.

Michael
what?

Audrey
the bloody lace, that's all nothing
I did it too tight

Michael
 let me see
 what's wrong with your finger?

Audrey's finger is bleeding.

Audrey
 I caught it

Michael
 on the lace?

Audrey
 its okay, I'll go for a run later

Michael
 the shoes look knackered

Audrey
 no, they're new

Michael
 they look like they have run a fair way already

He picks them up.

 let me
 soles all worn

Audrey
 I bought them last week

Michael
 then get a refund

Audrey takes the shoes back.

She looks at them.

She looks at the blood on her finger.

The window flies up.

Audrey
 shut the bloody window, would you?

Michael looks at her.

Audrey puts her shoes on the table.

She and Electra are on either side.

Audrey shows her the shoes.

Audrey
how did you know?

Electra
I didn't know

Audrey
when you said you had a message for me, I think you
knew the effect it would have

Electra
not at all

Audrey
stop playing games with me

Electra
I'm not

Beat.

Audrey
these are new trainers, I bought them last week
I haven't even used them but the soles are all worn

Electra
okay –

Audrey
I have been running in my sleep. It's obvious I have
been running in my sleep, you know I have been
running in my sleep, you seem to know everything
now, either I have been running in my sleep generally
or I have been running in my sleep after seeing
you again –

it means nothing that I have been running in my sleep
how did you know I was running in my sleep?

Electra
did they come after you?

Audrey
of course they didn't, Electra, because there is no them
that is what I have spent my life dedicated to proving
there is no them
there is only us
everything that we believe is external
is internal
it's a reworking of a painful emotion
in your case guilt

Electra
and in yours –

Audrey
my case is different

Electra
they said your father's name was Ian

Audrey
you know nothing about me

Electra
he's sent them to you like my mother sent them to me

Audrey
there are no gods, no gremlins, no curses
the whole of modern medicine proves that

Electra
why don't you do the talking?

Audrey
stop this, just bloody well stop this

Beat.

Audrey gets herself together.

listen, I am not going to play games with you
people can get a thing about their therapists
it happens often
we are trained to work around it
it is a part of the process
projection
you can project on to the therapist, the good bits,
    the bad bits, the bits that are too complicated, you
    can treat them like your mother for a bit, your
    father
your bloody abuser, your good side, your bad side,
    the therapist can be anyone
but I am not in this with you
I am not being hunted
do you understand that?
they are hunting you not me

Electra
you admit it then, I'm being hunted

Beat.

Audrey
of course you aren't

Electra
you just said

Audrey
a slip of the tongue

Electra
then why are you sweating?

Audrey
you are not improving
I was warned against seeing you again
we did this before, we moved on

it is only because I am starting a new job that I
    thought it would be clean, nice to see how you were
you were doing well with Dr Conway, I'll suggest you
    go back to him
you and I, I shouldn't have seen you again

Electra
either I am crazy, or they really are coming

Audrey
you're crazy

Electra
you don't think I am
that is why I bother you so much
that is why I bother you all

Audrey
you are a dangerous mind

Electra
listen

Audrey
that's the air conditioning
Electra, I don't want to have to call for a nurse

Electra
the window is open

Audrey
I'll shut it

Electra
don't shut it for me
shut it for you

Audrey
there is no need to shut if for me but because I can see
    the distress you are in, I will shut it for you
you are right, there is a memo on your notes saying
    the window should be shut at all times

She goes over and shuts it.

    it's shut now, I'll get the nurse to take you back to
       your room

SCENE SIX

Audrey is by the sinks, washing her hands.

She looks at her hands.

There is nothing wrong with her hands.

She looks at the soles of her shoes.

Jordan comes in.

Audrey
    you shouldn't be in here

Jordan
    I followed you in because you looked upset

Audrey
    this is the ladies' toilet, Jordan

Jordan
    if anyone hurts you, you know I'd do them

Audrey
    you should go back to the day room

Jordan
    what's wrong with your shoes?

Audrey
    nothing

Jordan
    you are the best you know.
    the best there is,
    we all say it
    there is nothing you wouldn't do for someone

Audrey
    thank you, Jordan.

Jordan
    you got a sweet?

Audrey
    I'll bring you one later

Jordan goes.

Fuck it, she thinks.

SCENE SEVEN

Electra is in her room.

Orestes is on a swing.

Orestes
    I was never any good to you

Electra
    too right there

Orestes
    I hate myself for leaving you

Electra
    you could have brought a fucking piece of rope for me
    that is what you could have done
    that is what most people would have done

Orestes
    you'll upset yourself

Electra
    so fucking what, so I upset myself?
    maybe I need to get really fucking upset for once
    maybe I need you to know how bloody screwed I am
    I can't run, I can't sit still, I can't escape

I can't end it
I am on my own
if there is a God up there, bloody help me

Orestes
oh fuck

Electra looks at him.

some fucker left the window open

Electra
what?

Electra looks.

She pulls on a bell.

The window flies up.

The winds outside howl.

the window
someone please get the window

Electra tries to stand up. She is chained to the bed.

She can't get far, she is straining to get away from the window.

can anyone hear me?
the window is open

All around her is sniffing.

Jordan comes in.

Jordan please
get some help, the window

Jordan wanders off.

Others are watching but are also useless.

someone

The sniffing gets louder.

    no, stay away

She tries to shut the window.

Her restraints stop her.

She can't get to it.

    Orestes, are you still there?

Megan comes in.

Electra struggles.

    the window –

Megan rings for someone else.

Megan
    there is nothing wrong with the window

Electra
    shut it

Megan
    you need air

Electra
    no, please

The sniffing and howling comes from all sides. Like a tidal wave.

Megan
    bite down on this, Electra

Electra
    but I can't

Megan
    I need some help in here, some preparation

Electra
    please just –

She is starting to thrash about.

    get them away from me

A second nurse comes in.

The Chorus come and watch.

Electra is surrounded by an imaginary pack of dogs.

    you'll rip me, you'll –

They are barking at her.

Twisting her.

Electra tries to fight them, struggling this way and that.

Two nurses and a doctor come in.

They get Electra into a restraint position.

She is struggling around, trying to get out.

The dog noises change to laughter.

There is laughter all around.

Electra rails at that too.

    no don't laugh at me

The nurses speak to her.

Megan
    no one is laughing at you, Electra

Clytemnestra's face seems like it is everywhere.

The laughing gets louder and louder.

Electra
    if there is a God, please end this
    God, are you there?

Electra is given an electric shock. From all sides and suddenly.

The world goes black.

SCENE EIGHT

Michael and Audrey look at Electra. Asleep.

Audrey
  she shouldn't have been given that

Michael
  we've had good results with electric shock therapy
    before

Audrey
  not with her, it didn't work with her

Michael
  we had nothing else to try

Audrey
  she is my patient

Michael
  not technically

Audrey
  we agreed we wouldn't with her again

Michael
  let's face it, some people –

Audrey
  one of the nurses left the window open

Michael
  so?

Beat.

Audrey
  it scares her
  scared her
  if she woke and the window was open

maybe it was our fault
there's a note that the window should never be open
    in her room, I think that should be looked into

Michael
oh you mean it is her own fear that causes this?

Audrey
yes, of course

Michael
because it sounded for a moment like you thought
    it was the window

Audrey
don't be daft

Michael
you won't mind my opening the window now then

Audrey
but she –

Michael
she's asleep
her brain shut down

Beat.

if it is her own fear and she is asleep
this room is a little stuffy, I think we could all do with
    some air

Audrey
okay, sure

Michael
okay

He starts to walk towards the window.

Audrey
don't

Michael
Audrey

Audrey
she had a bad night, can't we leave it at that?

Michael
not until you open the window

Audrey
I'm not frightened of anything

Michael
like hell you aren't

Audrey
you don't know anything

Michael
so open the window

Beat.

Michael
I know a grown woman, a top brain, someone
destined to be a leader in her field won't open
a window
that's what I know.

Audrey
I will open it

Michael
then go ahead

Audrey goes over to it.

She opens it.

Nothing happens.

Audrey
there you see, open

Michael
good

Audrey
you'll leave me alone now?

She shuts it again.

Michael
why not leave it open?

Audrey
it's cold

Michael
it's the middle of summer
hot I would say

She opens it again.

Just a little.

we went through this at the time
there is no such thing as a curse

Audrey
have you actually got a reason to be in here?

Michael
we all have patients we can't cure, people who are too
like ourselves

Audrey
only this isn't either of our offices and I don't think
this conversation –

Michael
alright
but she is like your shadow, and you need to let her go.

He goes.

SCENE NINE

Later, Audrey is on her own.

She is in front of the window.

She opens it.

Nothing happens.

She shuts it again.

She takes a deep breath.

She opens it.

Nothing.

Then a sniffing sound.

She listens.

She shuts it.

Song from the Chorus. The cracks in the window. The cracks in the glass. The cracks in the ceiling, the cracks in the house.

The cracks in the face that can't be put on in the morning.

The cracks in the woman who is falling apart.

SCENE TEN

Audrey and Electra.

Electra is talking now.

Audrey is in the wood, and Electra is at the side narrating to Audrey what is happening.

Audrey
    you are in a wood –

Electra
yes

Audrey
and she is in front of you

Electra
to one side

Audrey
yes okay to one side
always in the same place?

Electra
pretty much

Audrey
she looks like she is smiling, laughing

She can see Clytemnestra is front of her.

Electra
well not laughing, sort of –
it's hard to tell
when I'm there the pain –

Audrey
a physical pain?

Electra
above the ribs, but sort of spreading out across the
back

Audrey
as if you feel her wounds
does she talk?

Electra
sometimes, sometimes she just looks at me
I see her bleeding

Audrey
do you feel anything?

Electra
I hear the sniffing, the noises from them

Audrey
where from?

Electra
behind
she says they will hunt me

Audrey
and it's her that sends them, you're sure?

Electra
it isn't guilt

Audrey
I'm not saying it is anything I am just asking questions
I have to ask questions Electra, that is my job

Electra
next I'm on the mountain
there was a mountain that we used to go to. I'm there
with my father.

Audrey
okay, we're on a mountain

Electra
I never really met my father, but somehow –

Audrey
where is he in relation to you?
physically?

Electra
in front of me

Audrey
ah, I see
dressed, always the same?

Electra
>in his armour
>I guess that doesn't make sense either
>he was killed in the nude

Audrey
>its not supposed to make sense, go on

Electra
>he's angry, about Mum. He's shouting saying I have
>to this and that, fight and avenge. He says she was
>always evil, he gives me a ribbon from his wrist

Audrey
>a ribbon?

Electra
>yes, always the same

Agamemnon gives a ribbon to Audrey.

>it's supposed to keep evil spirits away

Audrey
>and does it?

Electra
>obviously not

Audrey takes the ribbon.

She looks at it.

Beat.

It not a ribbon, it's a bouncy ball. She drops it.

She stumbles slightly.

>can we go on?

Audrey
>yes. I just –
>are you sure it's a ribbon?

Electra
 yep

Audrey
 and always blue?

She stands out and pours herself a glass of water from a jug.

 just a moment

She stands and drinks the water.

She shakes herself slightly. She goes back in.

 and next?

Electra
 next is my brother

Audrey
 the same three always in the same order?

Electra
 when I see him then I know it's about to start
 that hell is coming
 I think he and I should have shared them but somehow
   they just come for me

Audrey
 they always come after you have seen him?

Electra
 yes

Audrey
 where is your brother?

Electra
 on a beach sometimes
 sometimes in a garden
 my brother can be anywhere

Audrey
the last time then?

Electra
he was here on swing
like there was a swing in this room
sometimes he takes me in his arms sometimes he –

Audrey
I can't see your brother, can you describe him

Electra
like me
only taller
same skin
skinnier
younger now
pretty useless

A little boy, Owen, comes in. He is about eight. He has a bouncy ball with him.

Audrey
now wait a minute

Electra
something wrong?

Audrey
you don't belong in this

Owen
fifteen bounces and I break my record

Electra
what's happening?

Audrey
nothing, keep talking, your brother

Electra
my brother is the only one that talks to me like he
knows me

The voice of an older man, Ian, starts.

Ian
you didn't even see him, Audrey, he was playing with
his ball

Electra
who's that?

Audrey
there seems to be something going on for me today
some crossed wires in my concentration
I am sorry, I think I'm getting a migraine

Ian
useless girl
he ran out behind me

Audrey looks.

Ian, drunk. is leering at her.

Ian
you want me to prove to you, you are fucking nothing?
and if you tell your aunt again

Audrey
can you pass some water, Electra, please?

Electra tries to pass her some water.

Audrey looks around.

and then the noises start . . .?

Electra
only if you hear them too

Audrey
you tricked me

Electra
how could I?

Audrey
I am your doctor, Electra, not the other way around

Electra
you said you'd never heard them –

Audrey
I dealt with it
I had years of therapy
I was fifteen, I was a mess, yes, but –

Electra
they never stop

Audrey
they did for me
they did stop

The sniffing is getting louder, the howling wind.

shit
will you ring a bell, Electra, will you get a nurse?
fucking hell.

The noises are all around her.

Audrey shouts at Electra.

what are you doing?
why aren't you getting a nurse?

Electra
you put me in restraints

Audrey
shout then –
wait
where have you gone?
Electra?
Electra?
Don't leave me in this
Electra?

Audrey is on her own.

She is frightened now. She looks all around her.

Her dad is in front of her.

Ian

I didn't do it

you tell anyone I did it, and I will fucking knock you
    to the sky –

Audrey

Dad –

Ian

I didn't do it

Audrey

there must be a way to make this stop

Ian

he ran out behind the car

I wasn't drinking, I hadn't drunk anything.

you were in the front seat and were playing with the
    handbrake

you're a little girl

nothing will happen to you if you say you were
    playing with the handbrake

Audrey

I can't lie

Ian

you haven't got a mother, what do you want to happen
    to you

you know what they do to children in care?

they eat them, they boil up their bones and serve
    them up

can you hear me, Audrey?

Her brother comes in.

He plays with the ball.

Owen
if I break my record, Audrey –

Ian
I was not in the car

Owen
he was drunk, again

Ian
fathers need help, Audrey, sometimes

Audrey
I am not seven any more, please

Owen
he was drinking at breakfast

Ian
I'm getting myself sorted, don't turn your back on
me. Audrey

Audrey
stop it
this is a hallucination

Ian
I've been going to my group

Owen
he is on the stairs

Audrey
I am a doctor, I am in a clinic

Owen
passed out

Audrey
some sort of projection, they are both dead

Owen
you are fourteen now, not a girl

Audrey
leave me alone
please, Owen
someone ring the bell

Owen
he's on the stairs, passed out

Ian
I need some help
Audrey, help an old man

Audrey
Electra, can you reach the bell?

Owen
walk over him, Audrey

Ian
I'm vomiting
I might choke

Owen
walk past him

Ian
if you do that I'll die

Owen
you and me we can get through anything

Audrey
Electra, is that you, has a nurse come in?

Owen
how many times are you going to clear up his vomit?

Audrey
Electra?

Electra manages to speak to her through the hallucination.

Electra
they never stop

Audrey
Electra, ring the bell

Electra
rope
that is what we need
rope is the only way out

Audrey
I can't do that

Electra
it's for us both

Audrey stops.

Audrey
get away from me –
get away from me –
this is not the way out

She pushes them away.

The noises come back.

The sniffing the barking, the laughing.

It feels so loud it's like your head might split.

Audrey is swirling around, this side and that.

YOU HAD STOPPED,
YOU . . .

The noises all around her become deafening, like hell itself has come to call.

She screams.

Audrey screams and screams.

Michael and Megan are talking over Audrey, who is now in bed.

Megan
you should have made a report if you thought she was in danger

Michael
what signs were there?

Megan
you knew her as a patient

Michael
years ago

Megan
but didn't declare it?

Michael
do people not get a chance to start again?
she got through it

Megan
her brother died in a road accident that she caused

Michael
no

Megan
there's a report
we all know about it now
she was playing with handbrake

Michael
she wasn't in the car, I believe

Megan
and then later her father died choking on his own vomit

Michael
yes I am aware of the details

Megan
if she was alone with him when he died
you should have come clean

Michael
I thought she had come through it

Megan
it's not my place but I would have thought you never
come through something like this

Michael
can't we keep it private, for a week or two

Megan
from the other staff?

Michael
this is Audrey
our brilliant star
this isn't just some patient

Megan
we'll have to move her

Michael
no, we keep her here

Megan
what about her new job?

Michael
I can't tell Ohio

Megan
she isn't the person they thought they were getting

Michael
she might get back to there

Megan
  she can't practise again, Michael, open your eyes
  do you want to phone Ohio or should I?

Michael
  can't we just leave it a week?
  do you have to look so fucking gleeful?
  this is someone's whole life going up the shitter, Megan
  I know there are things in your life that you are pretty
      bloody sad about, but must everyone suffer because
      of your pain?

Megan
  that's enough, Michael
  that is quite enough.
  I'll ring Ohio straight away.

She walks out.

Michael is left with Audrey, and his sadness.

He strokes her head.

SCENE TWELVE

Audrey is standing alone beside a window.

Electra is standing beside hers.

They aren't in the same space and yet somehow they are.

Audrey
  why did you never manage?

Electra
  I couldn't

Audrey
  fear?

Electra
    they wouldn't let me
    I tried
    I tried every which way
    I don't eat, I don't sleep
    I take the maximum-strength everything
    I have lived so long my body should be long over
    and yet I look like a girl

Audrey
    how long?

Electra
    an eternity

Audrey
    is that what is in store for me?

Electra
    I don't know

Audrey
    I was free
    I hadn't thought about them for years
    I was living my life

Electra
    they never go

Audrey
    they did for me

Electra
    they would have come back
    in the end.

She looks up to the top of the window.

    there is a piece of rope inside the window frame.

Audrey looks up.

    it holds the sash up

Audrey
  I see it

Electra
  can you reach it?

Audrey
  I think so

Electra
  go on then

Audrey
  but you said it didn't work

Electra
  if we do it together
  we are connected
  if we jump together

Audrey
  and leave this?

Electra
  it's not so much
  torment and misery?
  they won't let go, however hard we run

Audrey
  is it a curse?

Electra
  yes
  we're cursed

Both of them at the same time reach up for the piece of rope inside their window sash.

Electra
  if you can loop it over

Audrey
  are we dreaming?

Electra
  I don't know

Audrey
  they will have sedated me
  will have put me in a ward on my own
  Megan will have loved that
  I'll probably be at the end of the corridor, the one
    near the nurses

Electra
  take the sash, Audrey

Audrey
  we'll need to tie a knot
  make sure it will hold us

Electra
  no, we can just put it over our heads

Audrey
  we'll need a chair

Electra
  we've got chairs
  we've got everything we need

They both stand up on to the chairs.

They then put the sash around their necks.

They both stand there ready.

Audrey
  are you okay, Electra?

Electra
  yes
  are you?

Audrey
  yes

They jump.

A bell starts to ring.

There are bells all around.

They seem to come from everywhere and are really loud.

Then they stop.

Electra
we did it

Audrey
free

Electra
wait, what's that?

They are in a new place.

Chairs are being set up.

Electra looks around.

Audrey
maybe we are just dying maybe this is just the last bit
of brain activity

Electra
will it end?

Audrey
I imagine, yes, soon

Clytemnestra is in front of her.

Clytemnestra
it never ends

Electra
you –

Audrey
oh God

Clytemnestra
hell, Electra, is without end, that is the purpose
you don't get to jump free

Electra
my brother did

Clytemnestra
he didn't put the knife in my belly

Electra
it isn't fair

Clytemnestra
oh you want to argue with hell now?

Audrey
it's just the dying embers of your brain, don't panic

Clytemnestra
not true

Audrey
a final hallucination

Electra
please, Mum, let me go

Clytemnestra
it's not me, I told you

Audrey
hang on, Electra, this will pass

Clytemnestra
all that I can do is watch, even if I wanted to stop it

People start to walk on to the stage.

Electra
who are they?

Audrey
it's all in your mind

Chorus
clear a space!

Audrey
me?

Chorus
out the way

Electra
but I know you
you've been watching us all the way through

Chorus
exactly and now it's our bit

Electra
what bit?

Chorus
your trial
we're the jury

Clytemnestra
she doesn't get a trial, she has been condemned already –

Chorus
she made an appeal

Clytemnestra
what appeal?

Chorus
she appealed to god, I think

Clytemnestra
which god, when I got here I found there were none

Chorus
true p'raps, but Nature heard
you have to stand back

Electra
don't leave me, doctor

Audrey
I won't

Chorus
but your trial is later

Audrey
I get a trial too?

Chorus
not today but sometime from now

Clytemnestra
there must be someone who has got this wrong
what do you mean by Nature?

Chorus
older than the gods, and what will take over when
    we've all gone

Electra
so my case will be heard?

Clytemnestra
no need to celebrate

Chorus
it has been heard
that's why we watched

Clytemnestra
the ill-fitting, the insane?

Chorus
who better?
the left behind
the unseen
oh yes
the ordinary
who else could Nature trust?

One of the Chorus puts a box down.

Clytemnestra
you were deceitful then

Chorus
nah

Clytemnestra
said you were my friends

Electra
and mine

Chorus
we were watchers!
we watched, we didn't say anything
we didn't say much

Clytemnestra
you should have told me

Chorus
the votes have been cast anyway
it's time to weesht

Clytemnestra
I won't accept it whatever the outcome

Chorus
no choice

Clytemnestra
what is this?

Chorus
there is nothing bigger than Nature
that's what it is
the natural order of everything
death and rebirth
love and hatred,
you have to accept the vote
on one side, Electra is a window
you can't see it, but it is a window that will never shut
if the vote is counted and you are guilty, then there is
    nothing between –
you'll be ripped around and torn to shreds all night,
every night

Electra
is this still a hallucination doctor?

Audrey
I don't know any more

Electra
and what is on the other side, you said there were two
    sides

Chorus
is sleep, gentle sleep
a healing rest you crave

Beat.

Electra
I can see it, almost feel

Chorus
don't look Electra, not yet
even a glimpse of it will send you mad

Beat.

will you both accept the count when it's made?
there's no certainty of which way this will go

Electra
how many watched?

Chorus
you saw us six at first but another then another six
Nature called us, come and watch

Electra
tell us the results then

Clytemnestra
do I get a say, to put my case?

Chorus
you have had it
everything has been said and said again

Clytemnestra
   so we just wait?

Chorus
   while we count, yes

There's a noise.

The sniffing and howling.

   keep them back, we aren't done yet

Clytemnestra
   they are hungry, they want to play

Electra
   you only say that to frighten me

Clytemnestra
   why would I frighten you, this is hell's doing not mine

Electra
   it suits you though, this destruction

Clytemnestra
   shut up, enough has been said

Some whispering amongst the Chorus.

Electra
   is there a problem?

More murmuring in the jury.

Clytemnestra
   you said it would be quick

Chorus
   give us a second

Electra
   well how long?

The Chorus talk amongst themselves.

Chorus
    can we go back?
    I can't watch it all again
    and where would we start anyway?
    how far back?

Clytemnestra
    what's going on?

Chorus
    count again

Electra
    give us the news

Chorus
    you'll have to wait a little longer

Clytemnestra
    but the hounds –
    the window is already bulging

They count again.

Electra
    tell us what is happening?

Chorus
    how can it be, we are an odd number?
    it doesn't make sense
    as many on one side as the another

Clytemnestra
    count again

Chorus
    we have counted
    Electra killed her mother yes, it's obvious what should
        happen
    the child had no chance
    she should be punished

Clytemnestra
    quite right

Chorus
    I disagree
    she was never loved like she should have been
    shut up we've been through this
    if she'd had a proper childhood
    ach plenty don't get that – to take to murder?
    don't start arguing
    who said I am arguing?

Clytemnestra
    so there is no conclusion at all?

Chorus
    we're getting to that
    if the votes are equal then –

Electra
    what about the doctor, can she give a vote?

Chorus
    she isn't here, Electra
    she isn't part of this story

Beat.

Electra looks around. Audrey has gone.

Electra
    doctor?

Chorus
    she's gone,
    we can't finish then?
    no moral
    no conclusion
    bloody hell
    we've failed
    this restless house will stay stirring and vengeful

there must be someone else who can vote?
no one, who else could there be?
tell the audience, we have come to the end but there
    is no conclusion
that's rubbish
apologies
get your money back on the way out
sorry!
we couldn't decide
was Electra guilty or not, who knows!
can't we count again?
house lights up
perhaps a song, and they won't notice"
can someone pick up a guitar?

Clytemnestra
    what?
    this can't be it?

Electra
    and what happens to me?

Chorus
    I don't know, that's the whole point
    we can't finish
    the last scene will remain undone

Clytemnestra
    and me?

Chorus
    I guess you go back to the beginning
    do it all again?

A little girl comes on to the stage in a yellow dress.

Iphigenia
    excuse me

Chorus
    just a second

Beat.

Iphigenia
    excuse me
    can I get past?

Chorus
    where are you going?

Iphigenia
    to go and play

Chorus
    what is she doing here?
    this is a court
    we can't have children playing

Clytemnestra
    can you stop this?

Chorus
    is she part of the jury?
    who is this girl?
    you don't recognise her?

Electra
    she's Iphigenia

Chorus
    she was with us while we watched

Clytemnestra
    my baby?

Chorus
    Iphigenia. The first vengeful spirit
    are you sure?

Clytemnestra
    she should have the final vote

Chorus
yes, give her the final vote,
her death started all this

Clytemnestra
Nature sent her to finish it
and Nature would be on the side of mother and child
too bad Electra

Iphigenia
can I play here?

Beat.

Iphigenia sits down on the floor and opens the case.

Clytemnestra
stand up, Iphigenia

Iphigenia
but I want to play

Chorus
she brought Burdock for brutality
Bilberry for bludgery
I remember now

Clytemnestra
she sat on my back

Electra
exactly, she was your creature, that isn't fair

Clytemnestra
you have to choose now darling

Electra
remember I'm your sister

Clytemnestra
remember your mother's pain

Chorus
you have to be fair, Iphigenia

She stops. She looks around all of them.

She goes back to her case.

Clytemnestra
you have to choose

Chorus
you have to stay something

Clytemnestra
Nature has sent you to give the final vote, we've all
    agreed

Beat.

why won't she vote?

Chorus
is she going to sit and play for ever?
you were the first vengeance

Iphigenia
I wasn't

Beat.

Clytemnestra
you climbed on my back

Iphigenia
but I didn't

Clytemnestra
what?

Chorus
we saw you

Iphigenia
I didn't climb anywhere

Clytemnestra
I have the marks where you clawed yourself in –

Iphigenia
I did nothing
if you thought I did
it was because you wanted to think that
I am a little girl
Mum
Dad
Is my father here too?
I was a little girl
I wanted to play with my dolls
I wanted to run on the sand
I was never a spirit of anything

Chorus
but in your suitcase –

Iphigenia
there is nothing much in my suitcase
I was murdered yes, but I never came back

Electra
you spoke to me as well
you whispered words into my ears
Hibiscus, Hawthorn

Iphigenia
no
I did nothing
the living drive the living, not the dead
spirits and Gods and demons, we've gone
no lasting impression, no power to change
can I play now?

Chorus
you won't vote?
she's said what she has said
she can't say more –

Iphigenia
   my vote is for an end.
   it's to stop
   I was just a little girl
   everything else was you

Michael comes on, as if in a clinic.

Michael
   what is in your case, little girl?

Iphigenia
   you know my story?

Michael
   yes, I have your notes

Iphigenia
   in my case
   nothing really
   a little poultice that my mummy made me, that helps
      me sleep
   and a little picture of my dad
   and my sister is just a baby but she is here too
   and my brother

Chorus
   no Hibiscus, no Hawthorn?

Iphigenia
   I have a toothbrush and a hairband

Chorus
   no Bilberry, no Burdock?

Michael
   you keep them in your case?

Iphigenia
   yes I keep them all here

Chorus
   no Dandelion, no Comfrey?

Iphigenia
    just my dolls and my toys

Electra
    I remember now I had a case just like that
    I can't remember what was in it

Chorus
    poison and venom?

Electra
    not at the start, before it got emptied

Agamemnon
    funny, I had a case too, when I was a boy

Agamemnon has appeared on stage.

Chorus
    but you were always a warrior

Agamemnon
    no, there was a time before
    it was more of a box than a case but, in it
    if only I could remember –

Clytemnestra
    mine was a bag

Agamemnon
    I remember that

Clytemnestra
    you do?
    a little pretty bag

Orestes comes on stage.

Orestes
    there was never enough in my case to be honest
    it was always hollow

Iphigenia
there are things in mine
would you like something?

Beat.

Iphigenia gets things and offers them.

I've got lots of things. A doll or a ball or
a game we could play together?

Orestes
I can take something from you?

Iphigenia
why not, you're my brother. Do you want to play
a game?
I've got things for all of you.

Agamemnon looks at Clytemnestra.

you all need things, don't you? For you, Dad, a special
shell

Agamemnon takes it.

I stuck a nail through it but it didn't crack. For my
sister, plastic flowers

She gives some plastic flowers to Electra.

and for Mum a tin teapot and a plate of jewels

She hands these to her mother.

Clytemnestra
what sort of jewels?

Iphigenia
jewels I found by the beach
for you to put in your hair

Iphigenia holds up some seaweed.

Clytemnestra deliberates, she takes the seaweed.

then Daddy will tell you that you look beautiful and
you will smile. I have a teapot and five cups, I only
have water for the teapot but you can pretend it is
any drink you want

She hands her mother a cup. Clytemnestra takes it.

and you, Dad, will you drink too?

Clytemnestra
Electra?

Electra
Mum?

Clytemnestra almost falls.

Clytemnestra
it's hard, I can feel those creatures at my back

There is a sort of outbreath behind her.

Iphigenia
it's just a game

Clytemnestra
Electra?

Electra
we never played any games.

Agamemnon
forgive her, let go

Clytemnestra
as I am forgiven?

Agamemnon nods, then collapses too.

Agamemnon
I can't in fact, it's too difficult

Orestes
but possible, Dad, I am by your side

316

Iphigenia
you have to pretend it's tea
you can stir the sugar in if you like and pretend it is
    peppermint and then on this plate is whatever you
    can imagine

Clytemnestra
and us?
what happens to us?

Orestes
we just become ghosts, Electra is already dust

Electra
I'm dead?

Orestes
the rope held firm

Clytemnestra
and them, the creatures out there?

Iphigenia
I'll invite them in, give them tea. There is plenty for
    us all

Electra
no wait a minute

Iphigenia
they are only scary if you run from them. If you ask
    them in they sit down like friends. There is nothing
    to fear.

Michael
it's nearly the end of the clinic I think we've got
    somewhere
are you happy to close your case, little girl?

She nods.

Then I'll see you next time

A wind starts up.

He looks up at the skies.

   next time

*Michael gets up to go. He leaves the ghosts drinking
pretend cups of tea.*

SCENE THIRTEEN

Audrey is in front of a window.

She opens it wide.

Audrey
   fly away.

Jordan comes beside her.

Jordan
   are you okay?

She nods.

Audrey
   I wasn't

Jordan
   you wouldn't go anywhere, would you?

Audrey
   of course not
   maybe I came close but –

Jordan
   they said
   a patient died and if the nurse hadn't been there,
     you would have too

Audrey
   I know

Beat.

I'm glad she was there
that she found me in time
I watched my father die, and I didn't help him
I'll always have to live with that
but I can live
I can live with it
and look, the window is open

She looks out.

She leans right out.